TEACH YOUR
CHILDREN TO
PRAY

TEACH YOUR
CHILDREN TO
PRAY

BY

DENISE GEORGE

CHRISTIAN FOCUS

ISBN 1-85792-941-1

Published in 2004
by
Christian Focus Publications
Geanies House, Fearn,
Ross-shire, IV20 1TW,
Great Britain

www.christianfocus.com

Cover design by Alister Macinnes

Printed and bound by
Norhaven AS, Denmark

Contents

SECTION FOUR: The Perfect Example

SECTION FIVE: Creative Ways to Pray

SECTION SIX: During Family Distress

SECTION SEVEN: Holiday Prayers

SECTION Eight: From the heart

PRAY

FOREWORD
BY
CHRISTIAN TIMOTHY GEORGE

Babies spend a lot of time on their knees. For hours, they crawl on them, experiencing the world from a very humble posture. When they grow older, however, they learn the importance of standing to their feet instead of kneeling on the ground. But children *must* learn to return to those two knees. They must learn that there's more maturity in kneeling than standing. Children must train their eyes to read, and they must train their hands to write, but if those eyes are not trained to close, and those hands are not trained to fold, they will have an education without a salvation. Children must be taught to pray.

As a child, I learned to pray. They were not elaborate, ornate prayers filled with deep theological insights. They were not long prayers, polished with eloquence. They were simple prayers. They were the prayers of a child. I knew little about the world, the flesh, and the Devil. In fact, I knew little about *anything* at all! But when I opened my Bible to the book of Psalms and read how a shepherd would lay his sheep beside quiet waters, my eyes opened with interest. I knew a lot about lying down! And so I prayed, "Now I lay me down to sleep, I pray the Lord my soul to keep!" A prayer from a lamb who needed only the safety of sleeping by his Shepherd.

As the legs of that lamb grew a little longer, I managed to make it through the book of Psalms and even peeked over at Proverbs. Solomon seemed so wise, and I wondered how he acquired his knowledge. My eyes, somewhat older now, widened with wonder as they discovered a kneeling Solomon, praying for a Godly wisdom. I wanted to be a man like that one day, and so I asked the God above for a little wisdom down below.

He took me through the Scriptures. I met Joseph in his jail, and Daniel in his den, and Paul in his prison. I saw Jonah sitting in his seaweed and heard him wailing for a way out of that whale. Daniel prayed three times a day, and one day he spent an evening with a bunch of ferocious felines! I found that men of prayer struggled quite a lot in life! Christianity really cost them something! I realized that Christianity would cost me something too. Perhaps it would cost me *everything*! Could I afford to give God my all? Paul answered me well when he said how he considers everything rubbish compared to knowing Christ.

Everything I owned, including my faith, were all gifts given to me, not wages worked for. God, in His love, brought me to Himself. Prayer magnetized me to the Maker of Heaven and earth! When I bowed my head, I realized that a price tag hung from my heart, and I belonged to someone else. Bought with the blood of a Righteous Redeemer, I was not my own. Prayer tasted sweet to my lips because it reminded me of my helpless condition, and it pointed me to the comforting cross of Christ. My burden fell from my shoulders on that Calvary hill, and I began to thirst for secret moments with the Savior. I found in those early years a preciousness in prayer that remains to this day. Parents who teach their children to pray can be comforted with wise Solomon, knowing that "God hears the prayers of the righteous" (Proverbs 15:29).

When I was a child, I prayed like a child, but when I became a man, I found those prayers still powerful.

My parents taught me the mealtime prayer, "God is great, God is good, let us thank Him for our food." The older I get, the more I learn of His inexhaustible greatness. The longer I live, the more I taste of His overwhelming goodness.

Gratitude lacks the strength to describe how appreciative I am to my parents for their unselfishness in teaching my knees to kneel and my lips to pray. Their faithfulness to God in that decision molded me into a man who takes his burdens to the Lord, and leaves them there. For His glory, and by His grace, God has called me to be a preacher of His Holy Word. With my wife Rebecca prayer now forms the foundation of our new home, and one day we too will teach our children of its importance and necessity.

Every once in a while, when the waves of life distract me, and the distractions of life waver me, I'll think back to those early days when I first learned to pray. I'll see my father showing me the Psalms, and I'll hear my mother praying through the night. Even now, though I am grown, I fall to my knees like a little child with a simple prayer in my mouth for the Great Shepherd of my heart. The same God, who did not rebuke the little children as the disciples wanted, knelt upon the ground and hung them on His knee. Jesus taught our children something about kneeling that day! Jesus knelt for them, they should kneel for Him. When we go to Gethsemane to see the Savior kneeling on that stone, we kneel down beside Him and thank Him for dying on that tree. Children must be taught about that Calvary tree. For its root system will support them when everything else in their lives are uprooted.

Parents *should* teach their children to work in the world. Parents *could* teach their children to succeed in society. Parents *ought* to teach their children to follow their dreams. But if a parent wants to give their child the greatest gift in all the world, they *must* teach their children to pray.

Christian Timothy George - Son of Denise

DEDICATION

For Dr. Charles T. Carter,
retired pastor of
Shades Mountain Baptist Church,
Birmingham, Alabama.
Thank you, Charles,
our pastor and our friend,
for loving us, teaching us,
and guiding us spiritually
for almost ten years.
Our family deeply loves you.

SECTION ONE

WHY WE MUST TEACH

"GOD DID NOT CREATE US JUST FOR THE
PRESENT. HE CREATED US FOR
ETERNITY."
(DR. DANNY WOOD)

PRAY

MAMA AND PAPA

My grandparents taught me to pray. As a youngster, during my summer vacations at their home, I watched "Mama" and "Papa" open the Scriptures and kneel in prayer each evening. Papa prayed a prayer directly from his heart. He prayed for each family member by name and by need. By the time he finished the prayer, he had not only prayed for his family, but his neighbors, friends, community, country, and world. He filled his prayers with thanksgiving for God's good gifts, such as home and food and family and church and good health. Born around 1900, and married in 1919, during their lives Papa and Mama had survived two world wars, a great depression, the deaths of loved ones, life-threatening illnesses, and much more. They knew how to be grateful to God.

My grandparents were simple folks. They lived on a small farm in north Georgia. They loved their family. They worked hard for a living. They supported their church. And they had a simple faith. They believed

God's Word. They read it, tried to live it, and constantly shared it. And they prayed as the Apostle Paul told them to pray – without ceasing. Mama and Papa lived and breathed prayer. It was their very life-breath. And they taught me how to pray.

My grandparents, George and Alice Williams, have been with the Father for more than a decade now. I miss them still. Their photos grace the walls of my home. I constantly tell my own children about them. I appreciate all they did for me. Most of all, however, I appreciate them because they gave me the dearest gift – the greatest inheritance – that anyone could have given me. They taught me how to pray.

During those long, hot summer days on their small Georgia farm, I watched them each day as they knelt in obedience before God and thanked Him for providing their simple needs.

We must teach our children to pray because:
• Prayer education must begin in the home.
Suggestions for teaching your child to pray:
• Set aside time each day to pray as a family.
• Start praying early with your newborn child.
• Ask Christian grandparents to help you raise your child spiritually. If possible, invite them to join you as you worship as family.
During family devotions:
• Thank God for those devoted people He has given you. Let your child hear you pray this.

• Ask your children to help you pray for family, neighbors, friends, community, country, and world.

• Express thanks for God's good gifts, such as home, food, family, church and good health. Give your children the opportunity to add other "good gifts" to your prayer list.

Ideas to put 'legs' to a child's prayers:

• Find out who in your church or neighborhood is expecting a child. During her pregnancy, pray with your children each day for the development of the unborn baby. Put together a basket of baby powder, disposable diapers, baby lotion, etc., for your children to present to the mother when the baby is born. Continue to pray for this baby as he grows and develops.

AUNT MARY

My husband, Timothy, was an unwanted baby. At three months old he was more than his mother could handle. She boarded a city bus one day with her firstborn child, and tried to sell him to a stranger. She asked for $100 cash. Fortunately, there were no buyers on the bus that day.

When his paternal great-aunt, Mary Elizabeth, heard what had happened, she took the helpless and unloved baby into her own home, into her own tired, but loving arms. Old in years, exhausted in health, and money-poor, Aunt Mary mothered Timothy as her own son for many years. How he loved her! How she loved him! She could barely afford his food. Timothy's second grade teacher secretly bought him the two-cent carton of milk during "milk break" each day at school. Aunt Mary lived in a run-down hovel in a bad part of the city. She had no car, but, in all kinds of weather, she daily walked young Timothy to grammar school. By society's standards, Aunt Mary had very little to give a child. But she gave him her love, and she gave him the gift that pointed him to a lifetime of loving and serving God. Aunt Mary taught Timothy how to pray. It was a gift that money could not buy – the most valuable gift she could have given him.

I often reread the yellowed letters that seven-year-old Timothy wrote to Aunt Mary when his birth mother and father reclaimed him. They had heard that children brought government checks.

In the letters, Timothy begged Aunt Mary to come get him. The screaming, the fighting, the insanity in the new environment proved more than he could bear.

It was only after his father died in jail that Timothy returned to his beloved Aunt Mary Elizabeth. He was twelve years old.

We must teach our children to pray because:
• It is our God-given responsibility to teach our children to pray and to strive to develop them spiritually.
Suggestions for teaching your child to pray:
• Make prayer time the center, and the most important part of your family's day. Tell your children often how important prayer is to your family.
• Introduce by name to your children those devoted people who helped you develop spiritually. Pray for them together, and thank God that He brought them into your life.
• Have your children pray for those who live in poverty.

During your devotional time as a family:

• Pray for the unwanted babies in this nation. Pray that someone will adopt them and love them and teach them about God.

• Thank God for the world's "Aunt Marys" who give their lives to needy children.

• Study the lives of wonderful Christian women who gave their lives to help young children. Examples would be Gladys Aylward; Amy Carmichael and Mary Slessor. (Look out for the Trailblazer series of books as well as Lightkeepers published by Christian Focus Publications.)

Ideas to put 'legs' to your children's prayers:

• As a family, start a canned food collection. Provide a cardboard box. Each time you grocery shop, have your children select a canned food each to put into the box. When the box is full, through your community and/or church, donate the canned goods to help feed a hungry family. If possible, have your children help distribute these groceries to the impoverished.

PRAY

THE MARRIAGE

I loved Timothy the moment I met him on a summer Sunday evening many years ago. We met at my church, Flintstone Baptist. Timothy came as the youth preacher that Sunday evening. I was his convert! We dated almost a year, then married. We had a beautiful wedding in a small church in north Georgia with Mama, Papa, and Aunt Mary sitting on the front pew.

During the next decade, we moved far away from home, worked on educational degrees, and took on jobs. After eleven years of hard work and endless school, Timothy and I brought our firstborn son, Christian, into the world. For those eleven years, we had dreamed together about becoming parents. We had almost given up, but our dream had finally come true.

On the day of Christian's birth, Timothy prayed and penned a beautiful prayer to our new son: "Almighty God, Our Heavenly Parent. You have entrusted to us a life so fragile, so vulnerable, so completely dependent. We are afraid. How can we bear so weighty a responsibility? What if we make an uncorrectable mistake? What if we love too leniently or discipline too severely? What if... Free us from the fear of failure. Teach us that parenthood does not come like a cake mix – in four easy steps. Only in the daily doing of it will we learn the proper balance.

"Give us the grace to be good hosts. Remind us that this little one who will walk beside us for a few short years is only a guest in our home. We have no ironclad claims to his soul, body or life. Let us offer hospitality and kindness, gentle nudges and loving hands to mend the hurts.

"Sustain us in the storms of life. When we have reached our limit, when the world has done its worst, help us to say 'Into thy hands, O Lord, we commit it all.' In life, in death, today and every tomorrow, O thou who stillest raging winds, be near. Through Jesus Christ who was once a little baby, Amen."[1]

We must teach our children to pray because:
• Children need a life long, loving relationship with their Heavenly Father. They can accomplish this only through prayer.

Suggestions for teaching your child to pray:
• Tell your child about all the days you lived without him
• Tell him about how you eagerly anticipated his arrival. Thank God for him in his presence.
• Tell him about what being a parent means to you.

Encourage him to thank God for loving parents who care about his spiritual growth.

• Thank God together for the precious baby Jesus.

During your devotional time as a family:

• Pray a prayer especially for your child so that he may hear you pray for him. Be specific about his needs.

• On a sheet of paper, write the prayer and give it to your child.

• Reread the prayer often during your devotional times together. Let him know how precious he is to you.

Ideas to put 'legs' to your children's prayers:

• Pray daily for the engaged and/or newly-married couples in your church. Ask God to give them strong, lasting marriages that will become solid spiritual foundations for their future children. Have your children send cards of congratulations to these couples, and tell them your family is praying for them.

WELCOME, CHRISTIAN!

A whole new world awaited us when Timothy and I became parents. Neither one of us had had any experience with babies. In fact, neither one of us had ever changed a diaper! We honestly didn't know which end of the baby to take care of first! Should we feed him? Or should we change him? Earlier we had laughed when other new parents jokingly told us their definition of a baby: "a ravenous appetite at one end; complete irresponsibility at the other end"!

But we weren't laughing now.

We were completely overwhelmed with the responsibility that had suddenly become ours. We had a newborn baby who depended on us for his very life. When he got hungry, he screamed. When he wet his diapers, he fussed. He slept all day and kept us awake all night. He always wanted his own way, and he usually got it! I asked Timothy several times that first few weeks: "Now just what were those reasons that you and I wanted children?"

Tim Kimmel writes: "When I hear some misguided person discuss the cherubic nature of children, I have to laugh. They obviously haven't had any."[2]

Those proved long days, and even longer nights! And Mama, Papa, and Aunt Mary lived 300 miles away! We were totally on our own. And scared to death.

At first, I think we did everything wrong! The first shock came when we brought Christian home from the hospital. All went sweet-smelling and baby-powder perfect but then neither Timothy nor I knew how to change a diaper. Leaning over Christian's crib, scratching our heads in mutual puzzlement, trying to figure out how to diaper this tiny naked newborn, we stood there for the longest time. Too long. Before I figured out how to put that tiny Pampers on my baby's tiny bottom, my face literally "dripped" with surprise. At the "sprinkling," I saw a look of horror cross Timothy's face, and I heard him say something like: "I'm outta here!" as he ran out the nursery door. They never taught us these things in graduate school!

We must teach our children to pray because:
• If we don't, they will miss a major part of their spiritual upbringing.
Suggestions for teaching your child to pray:
• For very young children, keep prayer time short and simple.
• Let your children know that this is a serious time, but a wonderful family time, too.

• Explain that nobody is born perfect. But tell them that God loves us anyway, even when we make mistakes. Pray together that God will forgive all your mistakes – your child's and your own.

During your devotional time as a family:

• Laugh together over your new parent blunders!

• Let your child hear you reminisce often about your child's early days.

• Don't get discouraged if your young child seems uninterested or restless at first. Just keep on keeping on with family devotions.

Ideas to put 'legs' to your children's prayers:

• As a family, volunteer some time to help a new mother with her baby and/or household chores. You might offer to babysit, or wash windows, or take the baby on a stroll, or make dinner for them one night. Speaking from experience, anything you do for them will be much appreciated!

PRAY

NEW-DADDY-CLUMSINESS

We knew nothing at first about taking care of a child physically. But Mama, Papa, and Aunt Mary had taught us plenty about taking care of a child spiritually. So the moment newborn Christian arrived into his new home, Timothy and I carried him into our bedroom. Sitting in a comfortable chair, and with noticeable new-daddy-clumsiness, Timothy held our new son in his arms. He opened our family Bible to Psalm 1 and began to read God's Word to Christian.

"Blessed is the man that walketh not in the counsel of the ungodly," Timothy read from the King James Version, "nor standeth in the way of sinners, nor sitteth in the seat of the scornful. But his delight is in the law of the Lord; and in his law doth he meditate day and night." At three days old, Christian could hardly focus his eyes, but Timothy read nonetheless. "And he shall be like a tree planted by the rivers of water, that bringeth forth his fruit in his season; his leaf also shall not wither; and whatsoever he doeth shall prosper." Timothy and I then placed our hands on our sleeping son. Together we prayed our first prayer as father, mother, and child – the most important moment of Christian's life. For we had given him the very best we could. We had introduced him to God's Word. We had begun to teach him how to pray. The next evening, when Christian was again enveloped in his daddy's strong arms, Timothy read Psalm 2 and we prayed together as family.

We must teach our children to pray because:
• Even an infant will come to understand that family devotions are a special time together.

Suggestions for teaching your child to pray:
• Hold your baby while you pray with him. Allow meaningful touch to be important in family devotions.
• Look directly into your infant's eyes as you read from the scriptures so he will feel an important part of family devotions from the beginning.
• Time is limited with young children so at first read only from the Bible. As your child matures add other sources, such as daily devotions from magazines, ancient Christian writings, and contemporary authors. But always include scripture. Your child needs to know that the Bible is the center of your prayer time.

During your devotional time as a family:
• Smile. Let your infant know that family prayer time is a sacred time, but also an enjoyable time to spend together.

• Read through the Psalms, a different psalm each evening.

• If your child is too young to sit through a whole psalm, read two or three verses at each sitting.

Ideas to put 'legs' to your children's prayers:

• Beautifully wrap a gift Bible and give it to a new mother and father in your neighborhood who may not be a Christian family. Write the mother's, father's, and new baby's name in the front of the Bible along with the date. Have each child in your family write his favorite scripture verse reference inside the Bible.

WELCOME, ALYCE!

Some twenty-three months later, Timothy and I had our arms full when we brought newborn Alyce Elizabeth into our home and family. A beautiful daughter, we named her after Mama and Aunt Mary. Her first night home from the hospital, Timothy again turned to Psalm 1 and began reading, "Blessed is the man that walketh not in the counsel of the ungodly...." Then, as father, mother, son, and daughter – our completed family – we prayed.

Early on, prayer became a natural part of daily family life. As best we could, we read the Scriptures and prayed together each evening. Before we ate, we bowed our heads and thanked God for the food. Before a trip, we prayed together for safety. During Saturday morning walks, we thanked God for caterpillars, flowers, and the neighbor's dog "Trouble." We took every opportunity to talk to God with our children.

We have discovered that when children learn to pray early, prayer becomes a meaningful, instinctive part of their lives. They learn to pray spontaneously, depending on God as Friend, Father, Comforter, Encourager, Provider, and Director. Prayer becomes as natural as eating, sleeping, running, playing, and breathing. "If we think of prayer as the breath in our lungs and the blood from our hearts, we think rightly," writes Oswald Chambers. "The blood flows ceaselessly, and breathing continues ceaselessly; we are not conscious of it, but it is always going on... Prayer is not an exercise, it is the life."[3]

Prayer and breathing – the first became as natural as the second. I heartily agree with Martin Luther who said: "To be a Christian without prayer is no more possible than to be alive without breathing."

Christian and Alyce are now teenagers. Christian will soon be leaving home for college. Alyce is learning to drive. They are good kids. But most importantly, they are praying kids! I have been amazed at the profound impact a few moments of family prayer and Bible study throughout the day have had on both children. They have learned to pray naturally. And prayer has become a necessary part of their daily lives.

Donald H. Strong once said: "If faith, devotion, prayer, love for the Bible, and regular church attendance are familiar and well-worn garments in the family wardrobe, they will come to fit naturally and easily upon the children."

I agree.

We must teach our children to pray because:

• Early on, prayer must become a natural part of daily family life. When children learn to pray early, prayer becomes a meaningful, instinctive part of their lives. They learn to pray spontaneously, depending on God as Friend, Father, Comforter, Encourager, Provider, and Director. Prayer becomes as natural for them as eating, sleeping, running, playing, and breathing.

Suggestions for teaching your child to pray:

• Take every opportunity to talk to God with your children.

• Stop often throughout your day and pray a short spontaneous prayer with your kids. (This is especially valuable if you have teenagers.)

• Explain to younger children how God is a Friend, Father, Comforter, Encourager, Provider, and Director. He is praying to Someone who loves him very much.

During your devotional time as a family:

• When your second, third, fourth...children come, start again from the beginning with family devotions. Prayer time should always be geared to the youngest child. Make this child feel just as important as the firstborn.

• When you have more than one child, plan a few minutes each day to have separate prayer times with each. Gear your prayer time to the age of the child. This allows all the children to receive a few minutes of special, individual prayer attention with one or more parents. (This is especially important in large families.)

• Pray regularly as a family every day if possible. This lets your children know that prayer time is priority time.

Ideas to put 'legs' to your children's prayers:

• As a family, share what prayer means to you with another family in your church or community. Give your children special opportunities to frequently share their faith with others. This teaches them to witness naturally and easily to those around them.

PRAY

PARENTING ISN'T FOR COWARDS!

Timothy and I are not "perfect" parents. We've failed more times than we've succeeded. I've asked God's forgiveness, and my children's forgiveness, for unwise words and thoughtless actions, more times than I can count. I've wept many midnight tears. I've spoken when I should have kept quiet; I've kept quiet when I should have spoken. Human parents rearing human children is no easy job. Dr. James Dobson was right to title his book: *Parenting Isn't for Cowards!*

"None of us is perfect," writes Tim Kimmel. "Every parent makes mistakes. But there is an observable difference between a dad who acknowledges faith and one who lives by it...between a mom whose belief is a compartment of her life and one whose belief envelops her life. Parents must lay their faith on life's firing line. It needs to be visible, embraceable, measurable, and transferable."[4]

In spite of all I've done wrong, I deeply love God, and I dearly love my children. I hope my children know that my faith "envelops" my life. I hope they see a faith in me that is visible, embraceable, measurable, and transferable. I know how essential prayer and faith has been to me. And I want my children to have the gift of prayer and faith that was given to me as a child. For they have sustained me for a lifetime.

We must teach our children to pray because:
• Prayer will sustain your children for a lifetime.

Suggestions for teaching your child to pray:
• Let your children hear you ask God's forgiveness for your daily failures. Encourage them to ask God's forgiveness for their daily failures.
• Tell your children how very important prayer is to the Christian.
• Explain to them why you so dearly love God. Have them tell you why they love God.

During your devotional time as a family:
• Hug your children often.
• Take time to stop and answer their questions about God and the Bible. Be prepared to be amazed at how much they really do understand!
• Incorporate a few minutes of quiet, personal prayer time for each family member, as their ages allow.

Ideas to put 'legs' to your children's prayers:
• Explain to your children that people often make mistakes that society does not instantly forgive. From your church, obtain names of men and women serving

time in prisons. As a family, write cards and send them to these prisoners. Tell them your family is praying for them. (Use the church's address, not yours, as a return address.)

PRAY

WHEN WE FAIL AS PARENTS

As all parents, Timothy and I have weathered diaper-changing, potty-training, food-throwing, carpools, soccer games, ballet lessons, piano recitals, band concerts, Christmas pageants, birthday parties, etc. This year Christian got his driver's license. Like all children, Christian and Alyce have grown and changed; they have had wonderful experiences and they have had deep disappointments; they have succeeded and they have failed. Like all parents, Timothy and I, too, have grown and changed; we have had wonderful child-rearing experiences and we have had deep disappointments; we have sometimes succeeded as parents and we have sometimes failed.

But we have discovered that, in the midst of all our parental blunders, we have done at least one thing right. We have prayed. We have prayed *with* our children; we have prayed *for* our children, and we have taught our children how to pray. We have tried our best to plant our little trees "by the rivers of water," and we can only hope and pray that they will forever "delight in the law of the Lord" and prosper.

Debbie Smith, wife of Christian musical artist Michael W. Smith, and mother of five children, states it like this: "They're not going to be perfect kids ... There are going to be problems ... So we don't expect the miraculous. But we do expect that one day, when they walk out the door to go on their own, they will be walking with the Lord. That's what we want."[5]

We must teach our children to pray because:
• Imperfect people need prayer and forgiveness.
Suggestions for teaching your child to pray:
• Realize that no parent can be a perfect parent. Strive for perfection in your parenting, but when you fail, ask God's forgiveness and then proceed with your life. Let your child hear you pray for perfection and forgiveness.
• Have a few minutes before scripture reading and prayer to confess your wrongdoings. If your children have said hurtful words, or have committed hurtful actions during the day to each other, encourage confession and forgiveness at this time.
• If you have wronged your children in any way, be sure to ask their forgiveness. Then pray about it together.
During your devotional time as a family:
• Realize that parenting really isn't for "cowards." It's a hard job. Spend extra time in prayer alone with

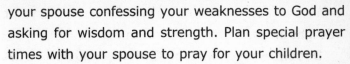

your spouse confessing your weaknesses to God and asking for wisdom and strength. Plan special prayer times with your spouse to pray for your children.

• Let your children hear you pray specifically for them. Call each child's name in prayer, and ask God to fulfill that child's special needs.

• Check and discuss often the spiritual atmosphere of your home. Do your children sense that God is the center of your lives? Do your children know how important prayer is to your family's life?

Ideas to put 'legs' to your children's prayers:

• As a family, plant a small tree in the yard of a new mother and father in your neighborhood. (Get their permission first!) On a card, write the following verse: "Blessed is the man that walketh not in the counsel of the ungodly, nor standeth in the way of sinners, nor sitteth in the seat of the scornful. But his delight is in the law of the Lord; and in his law doth he meditate day and night. And he shall be like a tree planted by the rivers of water, that bringeth forth his fruit in his season; his leaf also shall not wither; and whatsoever he doeth shall prosper." (From Psalm 1 KJV)

PRAY

WISH NO. I FOR MY CHILDREN

First, I want my children to know and to love God. I want my children to know that "God is closer than their hands and feet, and nearer than their breathing." When we pray with our children, and teach them how to pray, we open the door to their decision about their own eternal salvation. Since my grandparents taught me to pray, it seemed only natural that they also helped me to make the most important decision of my life.

Decades ago, on a hot August afternoon, as a gentle breeze blew through the back screen door, Papa and I sat together on the old brown sofa with our Bibles in hand. I had many questions, and opening the Scriptures, he had many answers. By the end of our talk, I was ready to make the life-changing decision. Together, Papa and I prayed, and I asked Jesus to forgive me, and to make me forever His. That afternoon, with Papa by my side, I committed my life to Christ in love and obedience.

Both Christian and Alyce have made this decision. Each child has willingly – eagerly – given his and her life to Christ. We have tried to teach them about God, the Bible, and our denomination's beliefs. But more importantly, we have tried to teach each child to know God personally. Not just to know *about* Him, but to *know* Him intimately.

We must teach our children to pray because:
• Children need to know and to love God. Prayer puts them "in touch" with Him and keeps them "in touch" with Him.

Suggestions for teaching your child to pray:
• Begin early talking with your child about his salvation. Pray together that he will give his young life to the Lord.
• Tell him how you, yourself, came to accept Jesus Christ into your life. Pray together that he, too, will one day make this decision.
• When your child is ready to make a decision for Christ, explain again what he needs to do, and then pray together with him. Contact your pastor to arrange for his baptism.

During your devotional time as a family:
• Talk about the difference in knowing about God and knowing God personally.
• If your child is ready to make a decision for Christ, ask your pastor to join you in your family's devotional time that evening. He may be helpful in answering your child's questions.

• Thank God together and rejoice when your child makes his decision to follow Christ with his life. Explain to your child why you are so happy with his decision, and what this decision means as far as eternal life with Christ.

Ideas to put 'legs' to your children's prayers:

• Let your child accompany you when you visit an unchurched friend. Explain the plan of salvation in Jesus Christ to your friend in front of your child. In this way, your child will learn to witness to his faith from your example. Encourage your child to witness to his own friends.

PRAY

WISH NO. 2 FOR MY CHILDREN

I want my children to do the work God has planned for them. When we bring our babies home from the hospital, we start them on a journey. When we teach our children to pray, we start them in the right direction. When a child comes to intimately know the Almighty Father as "Abba-Daddy," each step of life brings him closer to God. Through prayer, God will direct our children to find His purpose for them, His work for their lives. God's work is eternal. God will give our children's work its significance. Their life and work will have eternal significance in God's plan.

"I don't have desires for them all to be doctors and lawyers," states Debbie Smith about her children's future. "That doesn't matter. As long as they are where God wants them."[6]

What more could a parent want for a child?

We must teach our children to pray because:

• We want our children to trust God in their choice of lifetime work for Him.

Suggestions for teaching your child to pray:

• Encourage your child to call God "Abba-Daddy or Abba." Tell him what this name means.

• Pray together that God will direct your child in all his ways, and in his future work.

• Pray with your child, that the work he will one day do, will be eternal work for God.

During your devotional time as a family:

• Pray for your child's future.

• Tell your child why God's work always has significance.

• Discuss your individual occupations, and tell your children how you minister to other people through your jobs.

Ideas to put 'legs' to your children's prayers:

• Pray together for people in your church and/or neighborhood who have jobs that reach out and help others. (Doctors, nurses, ambulance drivers, firemen, rescue teams, ministers, etc.) Write each one a brief letter and thank him/her for the jobs they do for their communities.

PRAY

WISH NO. 3 FOR MY CHILDREN

Third, I want my children to strive for the eternal things of life, not the temporary things. I feel proud when Christian wins a soccer trophy and we place it on the fireplace mantle, or when Alyce writes a short story and it is published in a magazine. I beam when my children make good grades, or play their best in a piano recital, or take such joy in good music and good books. But however back-patting these accomplishments are, I know they are only temporary. They make us smile for a while, and they bring praise from others, but they will not last. I want my children to learn the difference between the eternal and the temporary. I want them to know those things that will last and those things that will not last beyond an hour, a year, or a lifetime.

Knowing God intimately, striving to do the work He has given us, and always reaching for the eternal that He offers us, are the things that will outlast this life. These are eternal gifts, not ones that will fade and be forgotten with time. Your children have souls that are meant to live forever.

"Faith is the foundation of our legacy. It enables us to give one of the most significant gifts of all to our children. It prepares them to die. Death is inescapable. There are no exceptions. So why not relieve our children of the burden? Living is a lot easier when we don't have to keep looking over our shoulder. Once we are prepared to die, we are free to live!"[7]

"God did not create us just for the present. He created us for eternity," my pastor, Danny Wood, puts it so beautifully. "Once we are prepared to die," writes Tim Kimmel, "we are free to live!" While my children are in my care, I want to rear them for eternity. I want them to know and to love the One who so loves them; the One with whom they will spend forever. When we teach our children to pray, we put their tender feet on the lifelong path of eternity.

We must teach our children to pray because:
• Death is inevitable. Prayer gives children the assurance that God is real and that, as God's children, heaven is their final home.

Suggestions for teaching your child to pray:
• Routinely tell your children your wishes for their lives. Pray that God will accomplish these.
• Explain the meaning of eternity, and how it should affect the way they live their lives now. Encourage them to pray for God's guidance and direction in life.

- Whenever you pray as a family, talk about eternity, and what it means to be a child of God. Tell them eternity starts the minute we accept Christ into our lives, and continues forever. Tell them they are indwelt with God's Holy Spirit when they are "born again" into God's family. Thank God together for the gift of eternity with Him.

During your devotional time as a family:

- Tell your children often your hopes and dreams for them as they mature.
- Share with them the details of your own salvation experience. Tell them what Jesus means to you and to your family's life together.
- Be spiritually-alert to your children. Be ready to talk when they come to you asking about their own salvation.

Ideas to put 'legs' to your children's prayers:

- Take your children to visit an elderly Christian person. Ask her to talk about her life, what she accomplished, who she loved, and what was most important to her then and now. Ask her this question: "If you had your life to live over again, what would you do differently?"

TWO THINGS THAT LAST FOREVER

There are two things that God tells us will last forever. The first is His Word. "Heaven and earth will pass away," Jesus said, "but my words will never pass away" (Matthew 24:35 NIV). Christ must be the foundation of our homes. If our children have no foundation, they cannot build strong sturdy lives. If they have no ultimate authority, they will be swept along by every cult and every wind of strange doctrine.

The second thing is the soul of your child. "I tell you the truth," Jesus said, "he who believes has everlasting life" (John 6:47 NIV). Paul writes in Romans 6:23b, "...The gift of God is eternal life in Christ Jesus our Lord." Our children are born to live forever, to live either with God or to live separated from God. To know that your child lives outside of God's loving presence will be an eternal tragedy. But to know that your child lives within God's loving presence will be an eternal triumph. It is an indescribable joy.

We must teach our children to pray because:

• We want to give our children a strong foundation on which they can build sturdy spiritual lives.

Suggestions for teaching your child to pray:

• Immerse them in God's Word. Memorize it, pray it, allowing it to direct and change young lives.

• Before each decision, let the children hear you ask aloud: "What does God's Word say?"

• Buy your child a Bible. Bibles are now published for every age group. Write his name in the front. Let him use his own Bible during family worship. When old enough, let him participate in the reading of Scripture.

During your devotional time as a family:

• Hold Scripture up as your family's ultimate authority. Make it the solid foundation of your home and lives.

• Read to your children often John 3:16: "For God so loved the world that he gave his one and only Son, that whoever believes in him shall not perish but have eternal life." (NIV)

• Discuss how to build a strong spiritual life.

Ideas to put 'legs' to your children's prayers:

• Make or buy a bracelet that holds four small block beads. (Can be purchased at some Christian bookstores.) On each bead, put a letter, so that it reads like this: "W W J D." Explain that this means: "*What Would Jesus Do?*" When your child faces a decision, have him refer to the bracelet and ask the question: "What would Jesus do?" Encourage him to share the bracelet with friends at church and school.

THE GREATEST INHERITANCE

One day I read an article in *Time* magazine about the computer-genius Bill Gates, who, had become the richest man in the world. "He has become the Edison and Ford of our age," *Time* claimed. But listen as Bill Gates talks about his wife, Melinda, and his daughter, Jennifer, and his personal beliefs about God.

"'Melinda is Catholic, goes to church and wants to raise Jennifer that way,' he states. 'But [Melinda] offered me a deal. If I start going to church – my family was Congregationalist – then Jennifer could be raised in whatever religion I choose.' Gates admits that he is tempted, because he would prefer she have a religion that 'has less theology and all' than Catholicism, but he has not yet taken up the offer. 'Just in terms of allocation of time resources, religion is not very efficient,' he explains. 'There's a lot more I could be doing on a Sunday morning.'"[8]

One day, Jennifer Gates will inherit her father's money, and she will probably become the richest woman in the world. By the world's standards, Bill Gates will have left her the greatest possible inheritance. But by God's standards, Jennifer Gates will have inherited nothing of great value. For money is temporary. It is not eternal.

Mama, Papa, and Aunt Mary had not even a fraction of Bill Gates' money. In fact, they often counted out pennies to make a purchase. But how much richer is the inheritance they left us – the gift of prayer – an inheritance far more valuable than mere gold.

We must teach our children to pray because:
• The gift of prayer is the greatest inheritance we can give our children.

Suggestions for teaching your child to pray:
• Take your children to church regularly for worship. Congregational praying will help your child learn to pray with other people.
• Explain to your children frequently why teaching them to pray is so important to you.
• With your children in your presence, as a couple, recommit yourselves to God and to each other. Let your children hear you pray for guidance in their spiritual upbringing.

During your devotional time as a family:
• Look up the word "inheritance" and let your children read the definition aloud.
• Tell your children what you believe is the most important inheritance you can leave them.

• Read together this scripture found in Matthew 6:19-21 NIV: "Do not store up for yourselves treasures on earth, where moth and rust destroy, and where thieves break in and steal. But store up for yourselves treasures in heaven, where moth and rust do not destroy, and where thieves do not break in and steal. For where your treasure is there your heart will be also." Ask your children to list the "treasures" they want to store up in their lives.

Ideas to put 'legs' to your children's prayers:

• Take your children to Sunday School, and encourage them to get involved with others. Tell them that Sunday School is a place where they can learn about God, and also a place where they can reach out in kindness and helpfulness to their fellow Sunday School members. If possible, get involved with your child's class. Get to know their teachers and church classmates. As a family, pray for these people regularly. (Young children love to have their parents involved with them and their friends.)

SECTION TWO

LITTLE EYES AND EARS

"PREACH OFTEN,
AND IF NECESSARY,
USE WORDS."
(FRANCIS OF ASSISI)

CHILDREN LIVE WHAT THEY LEARN

Children live what they learn. Their most influential teachers are parents and grandparents. Children learn what they are taught. They learn by watching and listening. Parents and grandparents are the primary teachers of young children. To a young child, they represent God, Himself. We, as Christian parents, must witness always with our actions.

This fact was never so clear as the day five-year-old Christian whispered to me across the Thanksgiving dinner table: "Mommy, is Granddaddy God?" I looked at my dad. Tall, reserved, dignified, robust, sitting at the head of the table and carving the giant turkey, I could understand why Christian thought Granddaddy was like God. Parents and grandparents do represent God to their young children. God has given parents and grandparents that responsibility – the duty of representing Him – during a child's formative years.

That's a scary thought to most of us. We know we aren't perfect, but our small children don't know that.

And the choices we make as parents today will have lifelong consequences for our children tomorrow.

"...We must *live* the principles of faith throughout the day," writes Dr. James Dobson. "References to the Lord and our beliefs should permeate our conversation and our interactions with our kids. Our love for Jesus should be understood to be the first priority in our lives. We must miss no opportunities to teach the components of our theology and the passion that is behind it. ...I believe this teaching task is *the* most important assignment God has given to us as parents."[9]

We must teach our children to pray because:

• You will influence your child more than anyone. He will look naturally to you for spiritual direction.

Suggestions for teaching your child to pray:

• Encourage your child to pray for people he does not know personally who made wrong choices, and have suffered lifelong consequences because of this.

• Encourage your child to pray for people he does know personally who have made wrong choices, and have suffered lifelong consequences because of those choices.

• Cut out newspaper articles of community crimes, and pray for the victim and the offender.

During your devotional time as a family:

• Ask your child to look up and read the definition of "consequences." Pray together that he will allow God to direct his choices.

- List some bad choices. Ask your children to list the consequences that naturally follow these. For example:

Choice:	*Consequence:*
Rob a bank	Be arrested and put in jail
Hit someone	Get hit back
Tell a lie	Punished by parent or teacher
Cheat on a test	Cheat yourself from learning

- Play the "What Would Happen If..." game. Ask your children this question: "What would happen if you..." Then suggest a good action. Let each child answer the question in his own way. This is a good way to teach them that their good choices usually have good consequences. For example:

"What Would Happen If..." Consequence:

You were kind to someone else.

They would be kind to you.

You gave some of your money to church.

People would be helped.

You told someone about Jesus.

He might accept Jesus, too.

You joined a Sunday School class.

You would learn about God.

Ideas to put 'legs' to your children's prayers:

- To your friends, and to your child's friends who have made difficult but honorable choices in their lives, write each a note praising them for making the right decisions.

A SMALL WINDOW

Parents are given a small window of teaching opportunity in their children's lives. Within the confines of that limited time, we must teach them to know God and to pray. When that window is shut, it is shut forever. What a responsibility for Christian parents!

If our children learn by watching us in our own spiritual lives and prayer lives, then we, as Christian parents, teach our children to pray by the way we live from day to day. We teach them to pray in a similar way in the way that we teach them how to drive.

I didn't realize it at the time, but every time we buckled Christian into the car and drove away, we taught him how to drive. Little eyes, little ears watched us whizzing in and out of traffic. He saw the speed limit signs, stop signs, red and yellow lights, as well as our courtesy to and/or impatience with other drivers. He watched how we handled the fender-bender (those little bumps in the car that happen to all of us), and with what attitude we responded to the driver of the other vehicle. He routinely saw how quickly we slowed down when we passed a patrol car "hidden" on the side of the road. He took it all in – the good, the bad, the ugly – and he filed it away for future reference.

Teaching children to pray works exactly the same way. Although extremely important, just praying with our children isn't enough. We must also set a prayerful example for them. For instance, how do you and your spouse relate to God through prayer? How do your words to Him sound when you pray? Do they depict demand or delight or drudgery? Do you petition God, but never praise Him? Do you address Him as your intimate Father and Friend, or as a stern and uncaring Authority who sends lightening bolts your way? Do you think of God as a sort of "magic genie in a lamp" who owes you His gifts and blessings? Or do you give Him the proper respect and awe and adoration He deserves? When you pray, what does the position of your body say to your little ones? Do you resemble the "hypocrites" Jesus talked about in Matthew 6:5, who "love to pray standing in the synagogues and on the street corners to be seen by men"? Or do you follow Jesus' direction and "go into your room, close the door and pray to your Father, who is unseen" (Matthew 6:6 NIV)?

By watching us, our children will sense the importance of prayer, whether we consider prayer a priority or an exercise to rush through. Not only do they watch us conduct our own prayer lives, but they stretch their necks and open their eyes wide to see how God will answer our prayers.

We must teach our children to pray because:

• There is only a brief window of opportunity to teach our children to pray, and we must take advantage of that time.

Suggestions for teaching your child to pray:

• On a poster board or some card, ask your children to draw a large window. After they color and decorate it, write in the window everything you want to teach them before they grow up. Share the "window of teaching opportunity" with them, and pray together that you may accomplish this task.

• Make a "prayer box" out of cardboard or a shoebox. Provide crayons and colored pencils and ask your children to draw designs on it. Keep its purpose a secret until your next family devotional time.

• On index cards, ask them to write down prayers for other people and drop them into the secret "prayer box." Once a week, read those written prayers and repeat your petitions for them. On the back of the cards, record how God has answered those prayers. Once a prayer is answered, put it in a separate box.

During your devotional time as a family:

• Ask a child to read Matthew 6:5, then talk about it.

• Ask an older child to look up in a dictionary the definition of "hypocrites." Discuss its meaning.

71

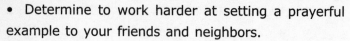

• Determine to work harder at setting a prayerful example to your friends and neighbors.

Ideas to put 'legs' to your children's prayers:

• Encourage your children to share the family's "prayer box" with their friends, so that they, too, might talk to the Father for them. (Be sure to share with others only those prayer requests that aren't confidential.)

PRAY

THE TERRIBLE HABIT I DEVELOPED

When my children started school, I developed a terrible habit. I so wanted to relax and watch the evening television movies that I found myself rushing through prayers and Bible stories with my children before tucking them into bed for the night. One eye on the Bible story, the other on my watch, I often failed to answer their questions and listen to their deepest heartfelt needs. As I am a morning person, by evening all I wanted to do was find a chair and collapse.

When Timothy brought this bad habit to my attention, we both knew I had to change. My night time movies were interfering with family devotions. And the programming was, in no way, enriching my life or the lives of our children. We made a joint and drastic decision to give away our two television sets. For seven years, we had no T.V. in the house. Only when Christian and Alyce became teenagers did we reinstate it. We now carefully control what we watch and when we watch it. And we will remove it again, if it becomes a problem. Spiritual teaching is hard enough without the world's influence streaming into our homes. Society makes spiritual teaching very difficult for Christian parents. Television is part of the problem.

We must teach our children to pray because:
• If we fail to teach them, they may never learn.

Suggestions for teaching your child to pray:
• If your family watches television, first pray as a family about the programs you watch.
• Before you watch a program, ask your children to ask this question: "Will this program be good for my Christian life?" If not, turn it off or watch another one, and together thank God you made that decision.
• Pray that television network heads/sponsors will upgrade programming to make it more suitable for families. Pray for writers to offer good Christian films.

During your devotional time as a family:
• For one evening, turn off the television set, and plan instead something special to do together.
• Write the sponsors of un-edifying programming and ask them to stop supporting that particular program.
• Write letters to those sponsors who support good family programming and thank them.

Ideas to put 'legs' to your children's prayers:
• If T.V. interferes with devotions unplug it, and get rid of it. As a family, pray for those who allow T.V. to distract them from worship.

CHRISTIAN PARENTING

When I was a girl (I was born in 1951), I lived in a different society than what my children now live in. Society helped my parents shape me and mold me into a God-fearing and God-loving woman. School and community leaders reinforced the Christian rules my parents and grandparents taught. The Ten Commandments were posted high on the cafeteria wall. Classes started with a Bible reading and prayer. Television shows didn't need to be "rated." Parents sent their children to the theater with a quarter and didn't worry that they would witness sex, violence, and crime on the big screen. In those days, on "I Love Lucy," Lucy and Desi (though married in real life!) slept in twin beds while on camera! Actors weren't allowed to use raw language in films. Parents, schools, and communities, for the most part, worked hand in hand to bring up responsible, spiritually-wise children.

"It used to be that parents, church, and school all spoke with a single voice," writes Chuck Colson, "exhorting the young to follow accepted moral precepts. Social civility was woven into the very warp and woof of people's character."[10]

The United States is a great nation. I'm proud to be an American. But while we have advanced quickly in technology, our value system has taken a giant step backward.

We must teach our children to pray because:
• Society will not teach our children to pray, nor will it support our decision to do so. Society no longer re-enforces the good values we try to teach at home.
Suggestions for teaching your child to pray:
• Pray together for the leaders of your country, pray that your nation would be a morally-sound one.
• Pray as a family that your and your church's life, will make a good strong statement to your community.
During your devotional time as a family:
• Explain how society has changed and why we should strive to become spiritually-wise citizens.
• Post the Ten Commandments on your kitchen wall.
• Reward your children for memorizing God's Ten Commandments. (Explain that society can take them out of their schools, but never out of their hearts.)
Ideas to put 'legs' to your children's prayers:
• Encourage lawmakers in your community to inject good values into their daily decisions.

TIMES HAVE CERTAINLY CHANGED

Times have changed! Now it seems that society is working against Christian parents who are trying to rear their children according to God's Word. Just look at what has happened in my lifetime: "In 1962 prayer was outlawed in public schools. In 1963 the Supreme court ruled that it was unconstitutional to have Bibles in public schools. In 1980 displaying the Ten Commandments in public schools was declared unconstitutional. In 1987 discussing God in the classroom was declared unconstitutional. In 1991 prayer at graduation ceremonies was declared unconstitutional. In 1992 prayer at sporting events was declared unconstitutional. In 1993 the state courts in Louisiana declared that teaching about traditional, monogamous heterosexual relationships was a 'religious' activity and therefore unconstitutional, even if there were no biblical references in the curriculum."[11]

Imagine! Society has removed the Ten Commandments, Bible reading, and prayer from our children's public world, and has replaced it with sex, violence, crime, gutter language, and unsafe streets.

What a tragedy. Somehow we, as Christian parents, for the sake of our children, must work hard to overcome society's lax moral code.

We must teach our children to pray because:

• Our praying children will grow up one day and make a difference in the world for Christ.

Suggestions for teaching your child to pray:

• Ask your children to pray for school teachers.

• As a family, decide which films to boycott. Pray for today's movie producers.

• Pray together that only godly language will be spoken in your home.

During your devotional time as a family:

• Explain to your children what bad language is and why we do not use it.

• Before you decide to see a film together, read a critique of the movie and discuss it. Pray that God will give you discernment in your choices.

• Tell your children that, as Christians, the Holy Spirit lives within them. When they put themselves in a situation to hear gutter language, they also subject the Holy Spirit to that language.

Ideas to put 'legs' to your children's prayers:

• Read the following paragraph to your children. Then ask them to write letters to movie producers asking that films be made without bad language: "I think it is interesting to note Walter Scott's response when a reader asked him: 'I liked [the film] "Ransom" but not the constant use of a four-letter profanity. Why is that word so special in Hollywood?' Walter Scott writes: 'For at least three reasons: First, many screenwriters sprinkle their scripts with that word because they lack the talent to write convincing dialogue without it. Second, studios prefer to make films containing violence and foul language because they earn an 'R' rating (and thus attract teenagers who shun PG and PG-13 films, seeing them as a sign of "immaturity"). Third, and perhaps most important, many moviegoers use profanity in their own speech and don't mind when it crops up onscreen. Indeed, profanity is now so accepted in American life that it's creeping into prime-time TV shows such as "NYPD Blue." Not only is this inexpressibly tacky, but it also cheapens us as a nation and a people.'"[12]

PRAY

THE RECIPE FOR 'SUCCESSFUL KIDS'

Family hour television often infiltrates our home depicting as good all those things we teach as bad. The message our children receive from society is: Crime pays; if sex feels good do it; virgins aren't popular; feel free to choose your sexual preference lifestyle; honesty is for wimps; there is no justice; women are sex objects; mothers and fathers aren't very smart; elderly people are silly and unneeded; religion is for losers, character is outdated, infidelity equals fun, etc. Children are constantly faced with conflicting voices – Christian parents versus a society that would make Sodom and Gomorrah blush. No wonder our children are so confused. If parents and grandparents fail to teach them about God, the Bible, moral values, and Christ's love, who will teach them?

"The day is long gone when we can leave the job to the public-school system or Sunday-school teachers," writes Joe White. "Successful kids (almost without exception) come from homes where a mom or a dad is teaching the basics of the faith daily, diligently, persistently, and lovingly...."[13]

Chuck Colson tells this story about 13-year old Tim and his school assignment who "... scanned his weekly quiz in Earth Science and read: 'Where did the earth come from?' Without thinking, he scribbled: 'God created it.' The next day, his test came back with a big red check mark and twenty points chopped off his grade. The expected answer was the Big Bang."[14]

No wonder today's school children are confused. No wonder today's Christian parents have a tough time teaching their children that God created the heavens and the earth.

Daniel Webster once asked Thomas Jefferson the patriotic question: "What is to be the salvation of our nation?" After a pause, Jefferson replied: "Our nation will be saved, if saved at all, by teaching the children to love the Savior."

We must teach our children to pray because:
• We want to raise "successful" kids who understand the basics of faith.
Suggestions for teaching your child to pray:
• Pray for current trends in society today.
• Pray that you, as parents, will teach your children about God, the Bible, moral values, and Christ's love for others. Let your children hear you pray this prayer.
• Pray for children who do not have Christian parents. Pray that they will somehow be reached for Christ.

During your devotional time as a family:

• Tell your children often that, in your home, you will strive to teach the basics of the faith daily, diligently, persistently, and lovingly.

• Explain what happened to Sodom and Gomorrah. Read the Bible story. (Genesis. 18-19, especially 19:23-25).

• With children who are old enough to understand, discuss the following dangerous and sinful myths of society, one by one, and ask for their opinions: crime pays; if sex feels good then do it; virgins aren't popular; feel free to choose your sexual preference lifestyle; honesty is for wimps; there is no justice; women are only sex objects;mothers and fathers aren't very smart; elderly people are silly and unneeded; religion is for losers; character is outdated; infidelity equals fun.

Ideas to put 'legs' to your children's prayers:

• Ask your child to write down the opinions he stated above, and share them with a pastor, church youth leader, Sunday School teacher, and Christian friends. Encourage him to ask for their opinions, too. (Hopefully these will strengthen his own convictions, as well as your family's convictions.)

PRAY

THE CHOICES WE MAKE

The choices we make today have consequences tomorrow. Not just for us as parents, but also for our children. Whether we *like* it or not, whether we *know* it or not, we are teaching our children about life, God, and prayer, by the way we, ourselves, live.

On his 16th birthday, I took Christian to get his driver's license. (He had been eagerly waiting for this day since he was two years old!) Before we left the car, Christian and I had a short prayer. I prayed that he might pass his test, and be a responsible driver.

Christian had spent the previous year "actively" learning how to drive. (Having a son who now has the freedom of driving presents a whole new ball game in parenting!) If I have tried to teach Christian anything about driving a car, it is this: what you do behind the wheel of a car will carry lifelong consequences.

"Christian, if you speed, you'll face police arrests and car crashes," I tell him. "If you aren't a careful driver, you'll end up hurting yourself and others. If you don't take care of the car, you'll be standing in the middle of a rush hour with a car that won't run."

When teaching my 15-year-old son to drive, I was very careful to mention all the potholes along the way. "Give the proper right of way to the other car. Don't drive too fast. Slow down when it rains or snows. Keep your eyes on the road. Never drive through a red light." On and on I coached him about good driving skills and the consequences that would result if he disregarded the rules. And he listened to me. Intently.

Christian now has his license but I have now discovered that a 16-year-old strongly resents his mother telling him how to drive. I thought my "good-driving-teaching window of opportunity" would be always open. But, alas, it has slammed shut! (Now, in order to get Christian's attention, I must remind him *whose* car he is driving and who buys the gas. I also remind him that I have driven more miles in *reverse* than he has yet driven in *forward*!)

When Christian buckles himself into "my" car and drives away, I silently pray: "Oh dear God, I pray that I taught him everything he will need to know about good driving. Please keep him safe. Help him to remember all the rules of the road. Please point him in the right direction so that he doesn't lose his way."

You see, I know that if Christian is careless in his driving, he will suffer terrible consequences. In some ways, driving a car is a lot like life itself. What we do in life will carry serious consequences for the future.

We must teach our children to pray because:

• The world needs our children's godly influence. They are tomorrow's adults and decision-makers.

Suggestions for teaching your child to pray:

• Write your names on separate slips of paper. Put them in a basket and stir them around. Each member then pulls a name from the basket. Keep the name a secret and pray for that person for a week. At the end of the week, ask each family member to tell whose name he drew, and how he prayed for that person.

• Ask your child to think back over the entire week, and then choose one event that made her most happy. Talk about why it made her happy.

During your devotional time as a family:

• Write up a list of your family's "rules for the road" for when the children start to drive.

• Using that list, write up another list called "rules for life." Let everyone in the family offer a suggestion.

• After Bible study and prayer, pull out the Scrabble Game, order pizza, sit on the floor, and have a friendly family competition. Adults may want to team up with younger children.

Ideas to put 'legs' to your children's prayers:

• Plan a time when you can invite a friend or family to dinner. Let your children help prepare the meal. After eating, invite them to join in family devotions. Ask your children to share their faith in Jesus with them. This will give your younger children a chance to witness to someone else in a comfortable setting.

PRAY

THE SEARCH

When my children began to crawl, I got down on my hands and knees and made a home-safety-search. Crawling through our house, I tried to see it through their eyes. What I saw shocked me. From their eye level, the view became dangerous. I instantly noticed enticing electrical outlets to stick my fingers into, long lamp cords to tug and bring lamps crashing down on my head, a bottle of bleach under the kitchen sink, sharp kitchen knives, and a kitty's litter box full of interesting things to touch and taste. Seeing their small world through their eyes turned my relatively safe home into the *London Dungeon*. I worried that my children wouldn't survive the first week of crawling! I immediately made some drastic changes. I plugged up electrical outlets with plastic tabs, removed lamps and cords, placed knives out of reach, and put the cat and his litter box into the great outdoors. I made the changes in my home that I knew would help ensure my infants' physical safety.

I wish now that I had also been smart enough to drop down on my hands and knees to conduct a "spiritual-safety" search. I believe it would have revealed many things in my personal relationship with God, my marriage, and my parenting, that would have also required some drastic and immediate changes.

First, I would have checked my own relationship with God through Jesus Christ. Would little eyes see me studying my Bible every day? Would little ears hear my personal prayers interceding regularly on behalf of them and others? Would little hearts sense my closeness to God or my distance from Him?

Second, I would have looked at our marriage. Did my relationship to Timothy come across as loving or strained? In what tone of voice did we speak to each other? Did my children see open affection between us? Or did they wonder if we were committed to each other and would stay together?

Third, I would have searched out my parenting skills. (That would have kept me on my knees a long, long time!) Did Christian and Alyce know that we truly loved them? Did they sense we were giving 100 per cent in trying to be good parents? Did they sense frustration, or hear irritation in our voices? In short, in those first few years, what did we teach our children about God? What did their little eyes see? What did their little ears hear? What did their little hearts sense? What we did as parents, and what we failed to do as parents, had consequences for our children.

We must teach our children to pray because:
- The world needs our children's prayers, too.

Suggestions for teaching your child to pray:
- Ask each member of the family to pray for each other's physical safety.
- Ask each member of the family to pray for each other's spiritual safety.
- Ask God together to take care of your home and to spiritually enrich the lives of each family member.

During your devotional time as a family:
- Let each child tell you why he loves Jesus.
- Ask each child this question: "What is the most important thing in your life right now?"
- Tell each other how you love each other and why.

Ideas to put 'legs' to your children's prayers:
- When you visit a maternity ward to visit a new born, remember to pray together with the new parents before you leave. Ask your children to pray silently for each baby in the ward. Pray for their health and happiness. Pray that they will each have a good spiritual upbringing with dedicated Christian parents.

SO MUCH TO TEACH THEM

Christian parents have so little time to teach so much! My children are almost grown now. I hope that as parents we have instilled good values, and taught them about the consequences of their actions. I hope we've taught character, fidelity, honesty, integrity, obedience, moral and ethical responsibility, sexual purity, and many other virtues. Windows of teaching opportunity close quickly. Surely the earlier we begin teaching our children about God and His Word, the more they will learn through that open window.

But above all else, I want my children to have a rich personal relationship with God. To build strong marriages and be faithful and committed to a future spouse. I want them to be responsible and loving parents one day, leading their children to love God, and teaching them to pray.

As a Christian parent, I hold to the wisdom of Proverbs 22:6. "Train a child in the way he should go, and when he is old he will not turn from it" (NIV).

I want my children to live happy, successful lives. But far more than that, I want them to be faithful and obedient to God, seeking His direction no matter what the cost. I want them to stand up for what they believe. I want them to know that the choices they make in life will have consequences, whether good or bad. And, when one day, they buckle themselves into their cars and drive away for the final time, I will silently pray that I taught Christian and Alyce everything they needed to know about living a Christian life during the years of training I had with them. "Dear God, Please keep them safe. Help them to remember all Your rules. Please point them in the right direction so that they don't lose their way."

We must teach our children to pray because:
• The earlier we begin teaching our children about God, His Word, and prayer, the more they will learn.
Suggestions for teaching your child to pray:
• Ask your child if he has any faith questions to discuss and pray about.
• Do a spiritual checkup. Discuss the spiritual atmosphere at home. Ask God to steady or increase it.
• Encourage your children to pray for faithful, obedient lives to God, that seek His direction no matter what. Tell them that this needs to be a lifelong prayer.
During your devotional time as a family:
• Twice a month, let your child choose a favorite scripture and allow him to lead the family in prayer.

• Tell your child often that you are proud of who she is becoming in Christ.

• During family devotions, be sure to openly and verbally express your love to each other.

Ideas to put 'legs' to your children's prayers:

• Ask your child to choose a person featured on the television evening news, and to pray for that person for a whole week.

SECTION THREE

TEACHING YOUR CHILD

"STORIES ARE DYNAMIC AND EXPLOSIVE.
THEY DO THINGS;
THEY CHANGE THINGS;
THEY MAKE THINGS."
(DR. TOM WRIGHT)

MY PRECIOUS JEWEL

Moments of greatest prayer, like moments of greatest motherhood, often come in plain packages. I was taught this, meaningful lesson, years ago on the morning of five-year-old Alyce's first ballet recital.

For months, Alyce had anticipated her first recital. It was her "big event." The ballet class girls, blessed with slim bodies and slender legs, laughed at Alyce's stocky thighs and thick waist. At five years of age, Alyce was a long way from society's ideal of a Barbie-doll, beauty-pageant figure! Alyce hid in the bathroom to change into her ballet clothes.

Alyce diligently practiced her bows and pirouettes. Still, they were awkward for her. "Honey, why don't you give up ballet?" I asked her. "It's supposed to bring you joy, not pain."

"But Mommy," she would say, "If I quit, I can't dance in the big recital." How I dreaded the recital! Based on Malachi 3:17 (KJV), the girls would dress as "precious jewels." I envisioned the graceful girls in pink sequinned costumes, and Alyce trying so hard to stay in step.

The morning was chaotic. Alyce's unruly hair refused to conform to a bun. We hurriedly put on mascara, powder, and lipstick. She looked like a little girl trying to play dress-up—which was exactly what was happening! Then we squeezed her into stiff slippers and an itchy costume too tight to be comfortable. Strands of hair escaped the bun, and tears smeared her mascara.

When we arrived at the recital hall, I noticed that the other parents (pros at these recitals) carried armfuls of long-stemmed, fresh roses for their dancing daughters. Tears filled my eyes. Was I supposed to bring roses for Alyce?! No one told me about this tradition. It was too late to rush to a florist and it looked like the other parents had bought every long-stemmed rose in Birmingham!

The lights dimmed, the program began. "And they shall be mine, saith the Lord of hosts, in that day when I make up my 'jewels,'" the speaker read. Dozens of little "rubies," "emeralds," diamonds," and Alyce, a pink sequinned "pearl," stepped onto the stage.

I said a silent prayer for Alyce as she danced the motions, staying in step with the girls. To my relief, the performance was uneventful. In fact, it was beautiful. Afterwards, throngs of parents greeted their exuberant daughters with roses. I had no choice but to greet Alyce empty-handed. When I explained my lack of roses she looked down at the floor and replied,

"I don't want to take ballet next year, Mommy." I felt my heart break.

Late that night, Alyce asleep, I saw something sparkle on the carpet. A pink sequin had popped off her costume. Picking it up, a sudden sadness enveloped me as I thought about my little daughter standing forlorn and flowerless among her peers. I slipped on my shoes and climbed into the car.

"Do you have long-stemmed fresh roses?" I asked a sleepy salesclerk at a cigarette-smoke-filled 24-hour drugstore. She looked at me like I had just landed on earth from Mars, shook her head, took a puff on a cigarette, and pointed to a bucket. "They ain't real, but that's all we got," she yawned. They would do. I woke Alyce that night and presented her with an armful of plastic roses and a note that read: "I love you, Alyce. I'm so proud of my little ballerina." For the first time that day, she smiled.

The pink sequin and cheap plastic roses have since found a permanent place on my bedroom dresser. They are a constant reminder that love and relationship and mothering Alyce are more important than all life's riches. They also remind me that most lessons in life are learned through everyday life. For these treasures are not made from silver and gold, and all that the world deems valuable. They come instead from everyday things. These are the silver and gold moments from which treasured memories are born, the little jewels of life that come in such ordinary packages.[15] Teaching our children about God's love and prayer also come in silver and gold moments... the little jewels of life that come in such ordinary packages.

We must teach our children to pray because:
• Prayer will uplift them in life when they need a Friend.

Suggestions for teaching your child to pray:
• Talk about how God works in ordinary, everyday life. Share with each other how wonderfully God meets your everyday needs. Name specific ways.
• Ask your children to pray that others will come to know Jesus Christ. Read together 1 Corinthians 3:6.
• Write thank you notes for your restaurant waitress. Pray for her before you leave the restaurant.

During your devotional time as a family:
• If someone in your church is elderly or in a wheelchair, offer to take them on a family walk.
• Write letters to homebound people from church. Pray for them. Let them know you are praying for them.
• Spend time separately with teens. Search out more in-depth Bible studies. In family worship time, each person should contribute and receive.

Ideas to put 'legs' to your children's prayers:
• Talk with your pastor and church leaders. Find out how you and your children can volunteer ways to help other people in your church.

ABSTRACT VERSUS CONCRETE

Jesus lived and walked and taught in the ordinary hours of everyday living. He took every opportunity – magnificent and ordinary – to teach people about prayer and faith and their heavenly Father who loved them. Jesus had a secret for teaching people about God. He took *abstract ideas* – intangibles – such as a neighbor's love, and turned those ideas into bone-and-flesh examples – *concrete stories*, such as the "Good Samaritan." What an exciting way to teach our own children about God and about prayer! As you reread the Gospels, notice how much Jesus used the "jewels of life" (concrete stories about everyday things) to teach those who followed Him. His stories came in such ordinary little packages, yet they contained the power and truth of God, Himself.

People, both big and small, infant or grown, love stories. It is no wonder that Jesus used this remarkable method of teaching during the time He lived on earth. People remember stories. People can understand stories on many different levels. From the earliest recorded days, Hebrew parents taught their children about their faith through story-telling.

"Stories are not just kids' stuff, pretty embroidery around the edges of serious abstract thought," writes English theologian Dr. Tom Wright. "Stories are dynamic and explosive. They do things; they change things; they make things."[16] We, like Jesus, can teach our children to pray by telling them stories.

We must teach our children to pray because:
• Your child may one day be the next Billy Graham!
Suggestions for teaching your child to pray:
• Thank God together that He gave us Bible stories so that we can better understand His Word.
• Choose one Bible story from the Old Testament, and ask your child to read it in full. Answer the question: "What is God telling us through this story?"
• Choose one Bible story from the New Testament, and repeat the process and question.
During your devotional time as a family:
• Have each family member share a favorite Bible story, and tell why this story is his or her favorite.
• Answer this question: "Why do people love stories?"
• Ask your children to share favorite stories not found in the Bible, and say why they love these stories.
Ideas to put 'legs' to your children's prayers:
• Tell your children the following story. Ponder its meaning together. Then ask each child what he can

do this week to show compassion to another person. "There is the story of an old saint who felt so strongly about the evil of the world that he prayed to God to send the fire of His judgment. He held out his hand in anger against the world and declared he would continue to do so until God made an end of this evil world. As he stood with outstretched hand a little bird came, built a nest in it and hatched her young. Bit by bit the saint became interested. Then his tenderness was awakened until the hand held out in anger was kept stretched out in love. God's patience with us is rooted in His compassion. In that compassion of God is the hope of a better world. In the compassion which His love can awaken lies our power to make that hope come true."[17]

PRAY

JESUS' PARABLES

We often call Jesus' stories "parables." Jesus takes his stories from the jewels of everyday life, something all people can understand. Matthew (13:34-35 NIV) tells us that "Jesus spoke all these things to the crowd in parables; he did not say anything to them without using a parable. So was fulfilled what was spoken through the prophet: 'I will open my mouth in parables, I will utter things hidden since the creation of the world'" (from Psalm 78:2). Even Jesus' own disciples pondered the use of his parables. "The disciples came to him and asked, 'Why do you speak to the people in parables?'" (Matthew 13:10 NIV). Jesus answers them (and us) in Matthew 13:11-17.

"I would have marveled at Jesus' parables," writes Philip Yancey, "a form that became his trademark. Writers ever since have admired his skill in communicating profound truth through such everyday stories. A scolding woman wears down the patience of a judge. A king plunges into an ill-planned war. A group of children quarrel in the street. A man is mugged and left for dead by robbers. A single woman who loses a penny acts as if she has lost everything. There are no fanciful creatures and sinuous plots in Jesus' parables; he simply describes the life around him."[18]

Small children to 107-year-olds (like my good friend, Friona Barnard) can learn from stories. Our education can be preschool or Ph.D. Stories cut across age, education, sex, and race barriers. Stories are like a song or a smile. They communicate truth, happiness or love in any language.

"The parables served Jesus' purposes perfectly," writes Philip Yancey. "Everyone likes a good story, and Jesus' knack for storytelling held the interest of a mostly illiterate society of farmers and fishermen. Since stories are easier to remember than concepts or outlines, the parables also helped preserve his message: years later, as people reflected on what Jesus had taught, his parables came to mind in vivid detail. It is one thing to talk in abstract terms about the infinite, boundless love of God. It is quite another to tell of a man who lays down his life for friends, or of a heartsick father who scans the horizon every night for some sign of a wayward son."[19]

We must teach our children to pray because:
• Jesus spent much time teaching His disciples to pray. Prayer is important to Him. Follow His example.

Suggestions for teaching your child to pray:

• Play the Bible search game "where is this story found?" and then ask a child to read the story: A scolding woman wears down the patience of a judge; A king plunges into an ill-planned war; A group of children quarrel in the street; A man is mugged and left for dead by robbers; A single woman who loses a penny acts as if she has lost everything.

• List some creative ways you can pray as a family.

• Pray that God will give your family members a hunger and thirst for His Word.

During your devotional time as a family:

• Answer the question: "How are stories like a song or a smile?"

• Discover why Jesus spoke in parables. Ask an older child to read: Matthew 13:10 and Matthew 13:11-17. Discuss as a family.

• Celebrate your children's good grades during family devotions.

Ideas to put 'legs' to your children's prayers:

• Invite your children to write their own "parable" and share it with a friend.

PRAY

USING OTHER PEOPLE'S STORIES

I love my daughter, Alyce, and my son, Christian. I would readily give my life for either one of them. I have a love for them that will never let go. They will always be my children, and I will always love them. No matter where they go, my love will follow them. Everywhere. Forever.

Jesus loves Alyce and Christian, too. He has already given His life for them. Jesus has a love for my children that will never let go. They will always be His children, and He will always love them. No matter where they go, His love will follow them. Everywhere. Forever.

Teaching children that God loves them is not always an easy job. You see, love is an abstract concept. We can't wrap our hands around it. We can't lock it up safely in a bank vault. We can quote them (and we *should* quote them repeatedly) this reassuring Scripture: "Who shall separate us from the love of Christ? Shall trouble or hardship or persecution or famine or nakedness or danger or sword?...For I am convinced that neither death nor life, neither angels nor demons, neither the present nor the future, nor any powers, neither height nor depth, nor anything else in all creation, will be able to separate us from the love of God that is in Christ Jesus our Lord." (Romans 8:35; 38-39 NIV).

Small children, however, may have a hard time understanding "trouble" or "hardship" or "persecution" or "famine" or "nakedness" or "danger." But through story-telling, this Scripture can be readily understood. For instance, in 1942 Margaret Wise Brown wrote the children's book, *The Runaway Bunny*. This amazing little "secular" book explains God's abiding love better than most "Christian" books I've read. And it probably doesn't even mean to! Filled with beautiful bunny pictures, Brown tells this wonderful story about a young bunny who threatens to run away from home. He says to his mother, "I am running away." His mother answers him with these words, "If you run away, I will run after you. For you are my little bunny." In Young Bunny's efforts to run away from his mother, he becomes a fish in a trout stream and swims away. But his mother becomes a fisherman and fishes for him. Young Bunny then becomes a rock on the mountain high above his mother. But his mother becomes a mountain climber, climbing high to where Young Bunny hides. Young Bunny becomes a crocus in a hidden garden. Mother becomes a gardener and finds her little flower-bunny. Young Bunny then becomes a bird and flies away. Mother becomes the tree that Young Bunny nests in. The story takes us through "Bunny Sailboat" and "Mother Wind;" through "Bunny Flying Trapeze" and "Mother Tightrope Walker," and on the story goes. By the end of the brief book, Young Bunny understands that no matter where he goes, no matter where he tries to hide, or no matter what he becomes, he can never outrun his mother's love and ever watchful eye.[20]

I think Jesus would have liked this little story book!

We must teach our children to pray because:
• God loves our children. He wants them to learn to hear His voice so that they may follow His direction for a lifetime.
Suggestions for teaching your child to pray:
• Tell your children that just as a mother loves her child, God loves His children.
• Teach your children to love others. Children watch society carefully. They see how society treats the rich and beautiful, as well as the poor and ugly. Somehow we must teach our children to love others by seeing them through God's eyes, not the world's eyes.
• Choose several people who aren't especially liked (perhaps someone in your child's school, or church, or community). Explain to your children that God loves these people even though they seem unlovely.
During your devotional time as a family:
• Talk to your children about loving others who are

different from them, especially those from different cultures and economic backgrounds.

• Purchase maps of the world, and pray for other cultures as you find them on the maps.

• Check out library books to study the habits and habitats of the world's people while you pray for them.

Ideas to put 'legs' to your children's prayers:

• Take ample time all through your day to pray for the world's people, learning to see them with God's eyes, learning to love them with God's heart.

PRAY

USING NATURE'S STORIES

We can teach our children about God, and the closeness of God through prayer, by using other people's stories. God's beautiful world around us – nature – also serves as a good teacher.

For instance, how do we teach our children about God's love and the incarnation of God through Jesus Christ. The "Incarnation" represents an abstract concept which some Christian adults can't easily explain. It's the Christmas story. The most often quoted "incarnational" scripture is John 1:1-5: "In the beginning was the Word, and the Word was with God, and the Word was God. He was with God in the beginning. Through him all things were made; without him nothing was made that has been made. In him was life, and that life was the light of men. The light shines in the darkness, but the darkness has not understood it.... (V. 10): He was in the world, and though the world was made through him, the world did not recognize him.... (V. 14): The Word became flesh and made his dwelling among us. We have seen his glory, the glory of the One and Only, who came from the Father, full of grace and truth. (NIV).

Sometimes these wonderful concepts are hard for young children to understand. Theological terms can be difficult and confusing. Just ask any first year divinity student! But through story, we can teach our children about God who came to earth in the form of a human being, and just why He did that. We can help our children better understand the "down-to-earth God," the God we celebrate at Christmas.

I once heard the beautiful, but somewhat sad, story of a little boy who sat at his bedroom window one night during a terrible thunderstorm. He watched as the lightning streaked the dark night sky and the rain beat hard on the roof of the adjacent barn.

During the most frightening part of the storm a small lost redbird flew against his bedroom window. Pelted by the fierce rain, the redbird began to fly in confusing circles, crashing again and again into the window glass, searching in vain for a shelter from the storm. Upset, the little boy ran out into the storm and tried to motion the bird into the safety of the warm protective barn. But the redbird didn't understand. He only became more afraid and confused.

Finally, the boy grew exhausted. He had tried, but he couldn't help the bird find the way into the barn. And the small redbird didn't survive the storm.

That night the little boy went to bed crying with a

wish in his heart. "If only...if only, for just a little while, I could have become a redbird myself, I could have shown him how to fly into the safety of the barn."

What does this simple story teach us? That God, Himself, became a human being just like us. He lived with us, and He showed us how to fly into the safety of 'the warm, protective barn,' the safety of God's love and mercy. He came, He spoke our language, and He showed us how to find life itself.

Abstract: "The Incarnation of God."

Concrete: "A little boy and a frightened lost redbird."

I often feel like Saint Augustine when I try to reflect upon and explain the incarnated God-man. For God is the "Gracious Mystery." We cannot explain Him. He is beyond explanation. Augustine felt so inadequate to explain God that he simply said: "I speak so as not to be silent." So touched by God through Jesus Christ, Christian parents also cannot keep silent, no matter how clumsy our efforts are. But a story helps. While no story can perfectly relate God's truth, even the best analogy breaks down at some point, children can easily grasp the love a little boy might have for a lost redbird. Using this story, we can try to teach them why God came to earth, and this deep love for each of us.

We must teach our children to pray because:
• While praying for others, our children learn to be compassionate, caring and to help someone needy.

117

Suggestions for teaching your child to pray:

• Teach your children about compassion. Compassion means: "to bear, suffer; sympathetic consciousness of others' distress together with a desire to alleviate it." (Webster's New Collegiate Dictionary, Springfield, MA: The G. & C. Merriam Co., 1981, p. 227).

• Tell your children that Jesus often showed compassion. Read some of the compassionate acts he performed. (Luke 13:11-13; John 5:5-9; Matthew 14:15-21; Matthew 12:10-13, and many other compassionate acts of ministry). Let them see how Jesus helped alleviate some of the world's suffering.

• Talk about the needs of your family, friends, school mates, church members, neighbors, etc. Have children think of ways they can reach out to help these people in need.

During your devotional time as a family:

• Plan to prepare and share a family supper with a new classmate's family.

• Have your children make and send a card to someone at church who has just had surgery.

• Encourage your children to volunteer to walk the dog of an elderly person in the neighborhood.

Ideas to put 'legs' to your children's prayers:

• Have older children volunteer to teach someone in the international ministry of your church how to read English.

PRAY

USING REAL-LIFE STORIES

We can teach our children through everyday newspaper events. I used this newspaper story to teach my children about the sanctity of each person's life. I told it to my school-aged children at a time when they were first hearing the word "abortion," but not fully understanding what it meant. First, however, I read from Psalm 139: "For you created my inmost being; you knit me together in my mother's womb. I praise you because I am fearfully and wonderfully made; your works are wonderful, I know that full well. My frame was not hidden from you when I was made in the secret place. When I was woven together in the depths of the earth, your eyes saw my unformed body. All the days ordained for me were written in your book before one of them came to be"(Psalm 139: 13-16 NIV).

I believe the following story revealed to my children just how precious each child is in God's eyes. (I later found out that, Rick Harris, is a member of our church.) 'Not long ago, about fifteen miles from our home, emergency medical technician Rick Harris failed in his efforts to save a newborn's life. A woman collecting aluminum cans had found the baby stuffed in a brown paper bag. Its umbilical cord still attached, the baby girl was covered with ants and barely breathing. She died soon after, and her tiny body remained unclaimed at the Cooper Green Hospital morgue.

When Harris learned that the newborn would be given a pauper's funeral and buried in the county cemetery, he vowed to provide her with a proper burial. "She came into the world hated," Harris said. "I wanted her to go out loved."

Harris contacted many businesses who donated money, a floral cover, a tiny casket, a burial plot, and a funeral service. The baby received the burial Harris had hoped for. But the grave site had no marker. And markers were expensive. But that didn't deter Rick Harris. He set up a fund to raise money for a proper marker. He raised seven hundred dollars, but that wasn't enough to buy the marker he wanted. With the further help of business owners and community friends, he was finally able to purchase the kind of marker he thought the baby deserved. But the baby had no name to put on the marker. So Harris named her Baby Hope, "in hope that the tragedy would be the last of its kind."'

Today, if you visit the Forest Hill Cemetery in Tarrant, Alabama, you will see the graceful marble monument. It is inscribed: "Baby Hope, October 19,

1988, Safe in the Arms of Jesus, Given in Love by E.M.T.'s and Friends."[21]

The monument is a tribute to a child who would have died without a name, a funeral, or a grave marker had it not been for a Christian man and a community who believed that every child of God is precious.

This tragic story of infanticide helped me explain to my school-aged children that every child conceived has value and worth. That every child "knit together in his mother's womb" has a God-given right to be born.

Baby Hope put a face on the millions of babies aborted each year, and helped my children better understand the evils of this monstrous, insane practice now legal in the United States.

We must teach our children to pray because:
• Unborn babies, as well as unwanted and unloved newborns need our children's daily prayers.
Suggestions for teaching your child to pray:
• Pray for society's pregnant unmarried teenagers.
• Pray for pregnant women who are considering abortion instead of birth.
• Pray for this nation's unwanted, unloved newborns.
During your devotional time as a family:
• Plan to spend some time at the local nursing home. It will bless both your children and the residents. Determine the needs of the people in the nursing home, and then decide on ways to minister to them.

121

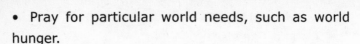

• Pray for particular world needs, such as world hunger.

• Serve your family a supper of beans and rice for a week when you focus on world hunger. It will help the entire family understand poverty in a new way.

Ideas to put 'legs' to your children's prayers:

• Help distribute food and clothes to the hungry and impoverished in the city where you live. Encourage your church to collect canned goods and used, clean, clothing. This makes a good Sunday school project for all ages. Take your children with you when those items are delivered to the families. Take time to get to know the families personally. Keep them on your prayer list.

USING WORD PICTURES

When we teach our children about God, we automatically teach them about prayer. Prayer is the way in which we come to know God. One way to teach our children about God is through word pictures.

Several years ago, the church where we are members, Shades Mountain Baptist Church, decided to build a new worship center under the direction of our pastor, Dr. Charles Carter. Our church members watched the structure go up with great excitement. The building was a dark mystery until one night someone turned the lights on inside for the first time. The bright light illuminated the large, magnificent window in the front of the church, sending lovely tones of rose, gold, and emerald into the dark night sky. On that night a mother happened to drive by the church with her preschooler. Seeing the lighted window, the child shouted with enthusiasm: "Oh look, Mother! The worship center's not even finished yet and Jesus has already moved in!"

To that little girl, Jesus was a bright light shining through the window of a dark building. What a wonderful image of Jesus, the Light shining bright in a dark world! Through word pictures and concrete images we can teach our children about Jesus.

"Jesus knew the importance of using word pictures with those who were timid of heart," writes authors Gary Smalley and John Trent. "He would talk about being the Good Shepherd who watched over the flock; the true vine that could bring spiritual sustenance; and the bread of life that would provide spiritual nourishment. By using everyday objects, He was able to penetrate the walls of insecurity and mistrust these people had put up, because stories hold a key to our hearts that simple words do not."[22]

Jesus often used word pictures to communicate to others. For instance: "Therefore everyone who hears these words of mine and puts them into practice is *like a wise man who built his house on the rock*...it did not fall, because it had its foundation on the rock" Matthew 7:24-25 NIV) ; "I am sending you out *like sheep among wolves*," Jesus said to his disciples. "Therefore be *as shrewd as snakes and as innocent as doves*" (Matthew 10:16 NIV).

We can easily picture in our minds these remarkable, yet everyday, images of houses built on rocks, sheep and wolves, snakes and doves.

These are just some of the word pictures from the Gospel of Matthew that Jesus used to communicate an idea. I could list many many more. With the use of metaphors and similes (word pictures) you and I can find new ways to teach our children about God and prayer.

We must teach our children to pray because:

• Praying is like breathing. You cannot remain physically alive without breathing, and you cannot remain spiritually alive without praying.

Suggestions for teaching your child to pray:

• Teach your child to be still and listen patiently for the voice of God speaking to his heart.

• Incorporate a quiet time of listening into devotions.

• Teach your children that listening to God is as important, if not *more important,* than speaking to God.

During your devotional time as a family:

• Ask a child to read Matthew 23:37: ("O Jerusalem, Jerusalem,...How often I have longed to gather your children together, *as a hen gathers her chicks under her wings,...*") Ask him what this image means.

• As a family, discuss the image of salt. Read together Matthew 5:13: ("You are the *salt* of the earth.") What does it mean to be the "salt" of the earth?

• As a family ponder together and then discuss the word picture "light," and the way Jesus used it in Matthew 5:14: ("You are the *light* of the world.")

Ideas to put 'legs' to your children's prayers:

• On paper, ask your children to write down six ways

that your family can be "salt" and "light" to the people around them. Incorporate into your next week some of their ideas for reaching out to others.

POURING IN ABSTRACT THOUGHTS

Children love photos. They delight in seeing people "forever frozen in time" at the blink of a camera shutter. Children can be taught to pray diligently for other people through a "prayer wall" in their bedrooms. Choose one blank wall in your child's room. Pin or tape photos of loved ones on that wall where the child can see them from his bed before going to sleep at night. Teach him to focus on one photo at a time, and to pray for that particular person. In this way, we can put a face on our child's intercessory prayers.

I constructed a "prayer wall" in my own bedroom. It helped me tremendously in my own intercessory prayers for others. In fact, each night before I sleep, I lie in bed and study my "prayer wall" of photos. Some are new; some are old; some are faded with age. But each person is precious to me, and each receives a special prayer before I close my eyes.

I love the people who look to me from my bedside wall. I pray for them with thoughts of love; I pray for

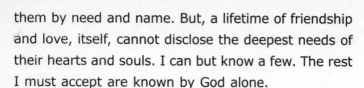

them by need and name. But, a lifetime of friendship and love, itself, cannot disclose the deepest needs of their hearts and souls. I can but know a few. The rest I must accept are known by God alone.

For all those needs unknown to me,
I ask that God will touch and tend,
My silent prayers to Him I lift,
The One Who is all-knowing.

Let us teach our children that a person's life is like a poem. A living, breathing poem. What is a poem? It is a collection of simple everyday words – carefully chosen words – a word here, a word there, each painting a portrait, each denoting a thought, each conveying a concept. If in photography, a picture is worth a thousand words, then in poetry, a word is worth a thousand pictures.

How can we make an abstract "poem" into a concrete image for our children? Let us tell them that a poem is like a small town's junkyard that whispers its unwritten history by the bits and pieces it leaves behind. Bits and pieces as of a puzzle, a puzzle that speaks unspoken volumes to those who will listen, to those who will look.

We listen and we see... The rusted tricycle of the child she never had... The worn crutches of a dream he had to forfeit... The dog-eared cookbook of a love she found and lost. For each person's life is lived full and empty. And we are given but a stanza, never the full verse of a life.

But God knows her heart, in and out and throughout the sonnet of her soul. He knows every thought, every fear, every desire. He knows her gain and loss, her hopes and dreams, her secret loves. He knows the ballad of her heart as He knows His own heart, without secret, without pretense, without the masquerade of a self-concealing mask. Thus, we hold the face – the photo – of the one we love before us, within our secret chambers. With words impassioned, we place this living, breathing poem of life at the faithful Father's feet. A prayer wall is a wonderful way to introduce your children to intercessory prayer.

We must teach our children to pray because:

• God knows your child's heart, throughout the sonnet of her soul. He knows her every thought, fear, desire. He knows her gain and loss, hopes and dreams, secret loves. He knows the ballad of her heart as He knows His own heart. She belongs to Him.

Suggestions for teaching your child to pray:

• Pull out the family photos. Have each child choose three, and pray a short prayer for each person pictured.

• Make a list of the prayer needs of the people in your church and community, and pray together for them.

• Ask each child to write a "prayer poem" to God. It doesn't have to rhyme, but it should be written from the heart. Read these together as a prayer to God.

During your devotional time as a family:

• Discuss as a family what is meant by the following: The rusted tricycle of the child she never had; The worn crutches of a dream he had to forfeit; The dog-eared cookbook of a love she found and lost.

• Construct a prayer wall in each child's bedroom.

• Let each child select his or her favorite photos to tape to the prayer wall.

Ideas to put 'legs' to your children's prayers:

• If you have a teenager who has just earned his driver's license, have a family party to congratulate him! This is an important "rite of passage" for a teenager. Ask the whole family to pray for his safety on the road.

PRAY

SOMETHING TO HOLD ON TO

"A person's life is like a poem. A living, breathing poem?" A poem is like "a small town's junkyard that whispers its unwritten history by the bits and pieces it leaves behind?" You see, we can give our children abstract thoughts – a person's life, a poem – and we can pour them into the concrete mold of a town's junkyard. A rusted tricycle, a pair of worn crutches, a dog-eared cookbook we can "see" and "touch."

When I was a little girl, my grandfather "Papa" poured liquid concrete into round molds and made patio steps. Before they hardened, Papa took a stick and wrote into each wet concrete mold the names of each of our family members and their birth date. (Some of my aunts didn't appreciate having their birth date in concrete for all the world to see!) Then he placed these patio steps around his yard. As a youngster, each time I skipped along those patio stones, I would "meet" and "remember" family members I didn't often see. Papa taught me to pray for our family members, one by one, as I hopped across their personal patio stones. You see, names and ages in concrete patio stones brought family members to life for me each time I skipped across those stones.

How I wish that we, as Christian parents, could write all of God's Word – all the abstract ideals and hard-to-explain theological truths – into wet concrete that would harden into permanent patio stones that would encircle our yards! Patio stones our children could skip across and each time learn and remember God's life-changing truths. When we pray for family, pull out the photo album, and put a face to those prayers. Post these photos on our child's bedroom wall.

Let us find tangible symbols to make God's promises come alive each time we see them. When Alyce asked me why the Bible called Jesus the "Lamb of God," I read her this Scripture: "The next day John saw Jesus coming toward him and said, 'Look, the Lamb of God, who takes away the sin of the world!'" (John 1:29 NIV). Using various other Scripture verses,[23] I explained to Alyce that Jesus died to make us right before God, much like the innocent lamb sacrificed in Old Testament days by the Hebrew people. I went into as much detail as her young age permitted. Then I bought Alyce a tiny stuffed lamb music box that played "Jesus Loves Me." When I gave her the lamb as a gift, I told her to think of Jesus as the Lamb of God every time she held the lamb and listened to its music. The lamb music box proved a visible reminder that Jesus loved Alyce so much that He offered Himself as a lamb sacrifice for her. The stuffed lamb served as a visible reminder of God's love for Alyce.

We must teach our children to pray because:

• God loves children, and wants them to communicate with Him. Prayer will change our children's lives.

Suggestions for teaching your child to pray:

• *Worship* God through hymns. Teach some of the old hymns. Many contain beautifully written theology.

• *Praise* God. Read some of these Psalms and let your family bask in the Psalmists' words of praise and joy. (Start with these: Psalms 8, 18, 19, 24, 27, 30, 33, 42, 47, 48, and include many others).

• *Thank* God. Everyone should answer this question: "What do you want to thank God for?" You will learn much about your children from this simple exercise.

During your devotional time as a family:

• Find three household items that, in some way, make God's Word concrete. Talk about them together.

• Ask an older children to read John 1:29 and explain its meaning.

• Sing "Jesus Loves Me" with younger children.

Ideas to put 'legs' to your children's prayers:

• Plan to do something kind for someone this week.

• *Genesis 22:1-19, especially verse 8 and 13*: The story of Abraham and Isaac. ("Abraham answered, 'God himself will provide the lamb for the burnt offering, my son.' And the two of them went on

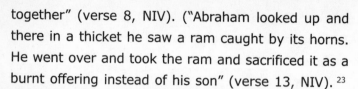

together" (verse 8, NIV). ("Abraham looked up and there in a thicket he saw a ram caught by its horns. He went over and took the ram and sacrificed it as a burnt offering instead of his son" (verse 13, NIV). [23]

• *Exodus 12, especially verse 21:* The story of the Children of Israel and the passover lamb. "Then Moses summoned all the elders of Israel and said to them, 'Go at once and select the animals for your families and slaughter the Passover lamb" (verse 21, NIV).

• *Isaiah 53, especially verses 5 and 7*: Isaiah predicts the crucifixion of Jesus. "But he was pierced for our transgressions, he was crushed for our iniquities; the punishment that brought us peace was upon him, and by his wounds we are healed" (verse 5, NIV). "He was oppressed and afflicted, yet he did not open his mouth; he was led like a lamb to the slaughter, and as a sheep before her shearers is silent, so he did not open his mouth" (verse 7, NIV).

• Also see 1 Corinthians 5:7; 1 Peter 1:19; Revelation 5:12 and 14:4.

PRAY

WHEN PRAYER PAINTS A PICTURE

Children love metaphors. With them we can paint a picture for our children. Jesus painted a picture to his listeners when he compared "heaven" to a "mustard seed." (See Matthew 13:31 NIV). What a strange comparison! But everybody in Jesus' day knew about mustard seeds, the tiny seed that grows into a huge tree. It almost seems that Jesus is being somewhat frivolous to compare something as mysterious and grand as heaven to an ordinary mustard seed. But he knew what he was doing. He was making a point, a point his listeners would long remember, a point that would survive some 2000 years.

How well Jesus used everyday examples to explain eternal truths! What a wonderful example he sets for us as we strive to teach eternal truths to our children!

We can teach our children about prayer using the same metaphor method. Ask a young child this question: "What is prayer like?" You'll be amazed at his answers. For instance: Prayer is like a bowl of hot creamy tomato soup. It warms up my insides on a cold winter day and makes me feel good; Prayer is like sitting by a campfire late at night and talking with my best friend; Prayer is like playing in Grammy's attic and discovering all kinds of wonderful old things; Prayer is like jumping into Mommy's and Daddy's bed when I'm scared in my dark room alone at night; Prayer is like being in swimming pool water over my head and seeing the lifeguard jump in to help me; Prayer is like sitting in my Daddy's strong arms and feeling safe and loved.

While these examples cannot even begin to explain the comforts, discoveries, intimacies, warmth, and mysteries of prayer, children can learn different aspects of prayer through these metaphors. This is a visual society so take advantage of that to teach your children about God and about prayer. Use every tangible object you can to help teach your children to pray.

We must teach our children to pray because:
• Praying to God will sustain your child when he faces disappointment and loss.
Suggestions for teaching your child to pray:
• Sing some old hymns that address God *directly* in a loving way. (Suggestions: "God, Our Father, We Adore Thee," "Joyful, Joyful, We Adore Thee," "How Great Thou Art," "Fairest Lord Jesus," and many others).
• Teach your children choruses you learned as a child so they can sing to God expressing their love for Him.

• Encourage your kids to write "love letters" to God. Save these letters to read (with their permission, of course) during future family devotions.

During your devotional time as a family:

• Play the game "what is prayer like".

• Sit down with your spouse and children. Talk about your own spiritual backgrounds. Did you grow up in a Christian home? Who taught you to pray? What did that person mean to you? Did your family worship God together at home, in church? What was the "spiritual atmosphere" of your home?

• As you examine your own prayer upbringing, list ways to use these ideas with your own family.

Ideas to put 'legs' to your children's prayers:

• Play the game "what is heaven like?" and ask your children to read out loud the following scriptures: Matthew 13:24: Jesus compared heaven to a man who sowed good seed in his field; Matthew 13:33: Jesus compared heaven to a woman who mixed yeast into bread dough; Matthew 13:44: Jesus compared heaven to a treasure hidden in a field; Matthew 13:45: Jesus compared heaven to a merchant looking for fine pearls; Matthew 13:47: Jesus compared heaven to a net that was let down into the lake and caught all kinds of fish. Ask your children to share these illustrations with your pastor, a grandparent, or a spiritually-mature friend, so that she can gain insight from them about what these metaphors mean.

PRAY

THE LITTLE RED WATCH

Something as simple as a preschooler's first red plastic watch can serve as a prayer teacher. I came to realize just how important tangible symbols are to the teaching of prayer on one chilly autumn afternoon. In fact, my children taught *me* a wonderful lesson about prayer that day. Earlier that afternoon as I spoke by phone to my friend Sara, my thoughts raced ahead to the minor surgery scheduled for me within hours. Sara faced a hard decision the next morning. "I'll pray for you, Sara," I told her as I hung up the phone. I grabbed my coat and purse and hurried to the family room where Christian, five, and Alyce, three, sat by a warm fire and drew pictures. "I'll be back before bedtime," I announced and gave each a quick kiss on the top of a tousled blond head.

"Is today your 'op-er-ation'?" Christian asked.

I nodded and pointed to Christian's new red wristwatch. "When the little hand's on the 5 and the big hand's on the 12 – that's when my operation is."

139

Than I added with a smile: "You guys remember to say a little prayer for me, OK?"

A few hours later, I returned from the doctor's office, sore and bandaged. With unusual excitement, Christian and Alyce greeted me. "We prayed for you, Mommy! We prayed for you!" they jumped up and down.

Timothy, who had not heard my earlier prayer request, chimed in, "I didn't know what was happening at first. All afternoon I noticed Christian looking at his new watch. Then around 5:00, he whispered something to Alyce, and together they put down their crayons, got on their knees, and started to pray aloud for you. I was moved by it."

I lay in bed late that night and smiled as I reflected on my children's prayer for me. And I also remembered an unsaid prayer, the prayer I had promised to say for Sara. I tossed back the blankets, got down on my knees, and prayed for her. In the morning, I would call Sara. "I prayed for you, Sara! I prayed for you!" I would tell her. Then I would go out and buy myself a little red watch – my own personal prayer teacher!

You may find, as I have, that when we strive to teach our children to pray, and when we watch their prayers develop little wings of their own, we learn more about prayer than we could ever teach them!

Surely, moments of greatest prayer, like moments of greatest motherhood, often come in plain packages.

A pink sequin, a plastic rose, a runaway bunny, concrete patio steps, an old photo, a town's junkyard, a little red watch – these are the ordinary things of everyday life that can make God's truths come alive – the "precious jewels" that can help us teach our children to pray.

We must teach our children to pray because:

• They will be teaching your grandchildren to pray!

Suggestions for teaching your child to pray:

• Teach your children to listen. Read Proverbs 18:13 and James 1:19 together. Only through listening can they learn to hear God's voice.

• Ask a teenager to read Matthew 18:20 and then explain it. ("For where two or three come together in my name, there am I with them" NIV). There is power in group prayer.

• Ask God to help you forgive someone who hurt you.

During your devotional time as a family:

• Let your children hear you answer these questions: What is your relationship to God? Are you as close to God as you would like to be? If your answer is "no," set aside time to examine your relationship with God.

• List ways you and your family can make your relationship to God stronger.

Ideas to put 'legs' to your children's prayers:

• Mail a card to someone who has lost a loved one, remembering the loved one's birthday, death date, and/or anniversary. Let someone know that you remember with love their own loved one.

SECTION FOUR

THE PERFECT EXAMPLE

"JESUS MADE PRAYER AND FELLOWSHIP
WITH THE FATHER THE PRIORITY IN HIS
LIFE. WHETHER HE HAMMERED A NAIL
INTO A BOARD, REACHED OUT TO HEAL A
MAN BORN BLIND, LIFTED SMALL
CHILDREN UPON HIS LAP, OR TOOK A
WHIP TO THE TEMPLE MONEYCHANGERS,
HE KNEW THAT GOD WAS
ONLY A PRAYER AWAY."
DENISE GEORGE

WHEN JESUS HIMSELF PRAYED

Jesus sets for us the perfect example of *how* to pray. He shows us how to approach our Father in loving effective conversation. Not until I read the Gospels over and over again, did I see an unmistakable picture of Jesus' own prayer habits. I was amazed to find that, while on earth, Jesus usually prayed in seven distinct ways.

Prayer was essential to Jesus. It was one of His habits (see Mark 1:35; Luke 6:12). The Father and Son had unbroken communion throughout Jesus' life. Jesus kept His heart focused on His Father while He worked, while He traveled, while He ministered. Jesus used to spend whole nights in prayer. He often got up before daylight and went out to pray. In fact, Mark tells us, "Very early in the morning, while it was still dark, Jesus got up, left the house and went off to a solitary place, where he prayed" (Mark 1:35 NIV). After His baptism, Jesus spent forty days in the wilderness, without food, to commune with God (see

145

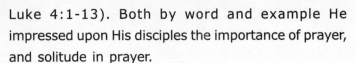
Luke 4:1-13). Both by word and example He impressed upon His disciples the importance of prayer, and solitude in prayer.

We can learn much about prayer, and how to teach our children to pray, from how Jesus prayed. He is the perfect prayer example to follow.

We must teach our children to pray because:
• "Prayer is not simply some necessary compartment in the daily schedule of a Christian or a source of support in time of need, nor is it restricted to Sunday morning or as a frame to surround mealtimes. Prayer is living." (Henri Nouwen)

Suggestions for teaching your child to pray:
• Teach them to pray for people who criticize them.
• Explain why Jesus asks us to pray for our enemies.
• Pray for someone who has lied to you.

During your devotional time as a family:
• Once a month, reflect on your prayer life together.
• Answer these questions: Do we spend enough time with God in prayer? How do we relate to God in prayer: Is He a loving Father or a harsh judge? Do we enjoy our prayer conversations with Him like we should?
• If you aren't happy with your prayer life, tell God what you wish your prayer time with Him could be.

Ideas to put 'legs' to your children's prayers:
• As a family, shop, buy, and deliver groceries to someone in your church or neighborhood who is recovering from surgery.

ONE: JESUS PRAYED INTIMATELY

"God made man for Himself, to be His child," writes Phillip Keller. "He created us with the incredible capacity not only to commune with Him, but to know Him *intimately* – to be His companions, conformed to His very character."[24]

Jesus prayed to the Father addressing Him as "Abba" or "Daddy." He prayed intimately because He had an intimate relationship with the Father.

Because of Jesus, we, too, can have an intimate relationship with the Father. Jesus described it as a shepherd with his sheep. We can know our shepherd intimately because he calls each of us by name.

Several years ago, I visited the Yorkshire Dales in England's countryside. Friends and I drove the narrow winding country roads through the rolling emerald green mountains. We found James Herriott's small dusty veterinarian office, unchanged after forty years, an office that spawned many wonderful stories and is now closed to both animals and curious visitors. Every few miles, we had to stop our van to open a sheep gate. After we drove through, being careful not to run over a lamb or sheep, we stopped the car and closed the gate. At one point, we took a walk among the sheep.

"I just want to pat one sheep's head," I told my friend, Ann. But, as I singled out a sheep and took a small step forward, the sheep took a giant step backward and ran away. We were strangers, and, as dumb as I've read they are, sheep are smart enough not to trust strangers. I pursued one sheep after another, all with the same frustrating results. Finally, I eyed one sheep that eyed me back! "Aha!" I thought, "this is the one." I stepped closer, and to my amazement and joy, it just stood there. Eyeing me. Unmoving. I took another step, then another. The beast slightly bowed his head, his eyes locked into a frozen gaze with mine. I stretched out my hand, and planned to move closer, when Ann called out to me: "Hey Denise! Know why they call that particular sheep a RAM?!" At that point, I turned around and ran.

I made two remarkable discoveries that day in a green English pasture, while standing among a flock of sheep and one very unhappy ram.

1. One doesn't fool around with rams, and

2. Sheep follow only their shepherd. They run away from pushy strangers with Southern accents.

Later, when I reflected on John 10, it all became very clear to me. Jesus calls Himself the Shepherd of the sheep. "...The sheep listen to His [Jesus'] voice. He calls His own sheep by name and leads them out. When He has brought out all His own, He goes on ahead of them, and His sheep follow Him because they know His voice. *But they will never follow a stranger; in fact, they will run away from him because they do not recognize a stranger's voice*." Jesus later says: "I am the good Shepherd; I know My sheep and My sheep know Me...and I lay down My life for the sheep" (verses 3-5 and 14-15 NIV, emphasis mine).

The shepherd is special to the sheep. The sheep listen for his voice, and they trust him with their very lives. They follow him wherever he leads them because they know him.

Likewise, the sheep are special to the shepherd. While the "hired hand" runs away when he sees the wolf coming, and cares nothing for the sheep (see John 13:12-13), the Good Shepherd leads, protects, and will even lay down his own life for his sheep.

Can we, the sheep, have that same kind of loving, trusting relationship with Jesus, our Shepherd?

Yes! We can!

You see, prayer is not something we DO – it is not just carefully chosen words targeted toward heaven – the variety of words that would make our English teacher proud.

Prayer is a relationship – a loving, trusting relationship – with God through Jesus Christ. We trust Jesus, our Shepherd. We listen prayerfully for His voice.

We know His voice, and we follow Him wherever He leads us. Likewise, Jesus loves us so much that He willingly laid down His life for us, His lambs. By teaching our children about the relationship between the shepherd and his sheep, we can teach them about the kind of prayer God intends for us to enjoy.

Phillip Keller also writes: "The incredibly beautiful relationship between the Shepherd and His sheep can be and only is possible provided the sheep hear His voice, are known of Him in intimate oneness, and so follow Him in quiet, implicit confidence."[25]

Jesus gave His life so that you and I can have an intimate prayer relationship with God. When we pray to the Father, we, too, can call Him "Abba—Daddy." When we pray with our children, let us often address our Father as "Abba-Daddy."

We must teach our children to pray because:
• Jesus gave His life so that you and I can have an intimate prayer relationship with God.

Suggestions for teaching your child to pray:
• During your prayer time together, be sensitive to the Spirit so that you may gain valuable insight in how to pray. Read together Acts 13:1-3.
• Invite a lonely friend out to lunch. Pray daily for her.
• Pray for the people in your community and church who cannot read or write. Offer to read Bible stories and books to their children.

During your devotional time as a family:

• Look up the word "intimate" in your dictionary and talk about its meaning.

• Evaluate your relationship with your spouse and children. Do you pray regularly for each other? Are you each seeking to become spiritual soul mates for each other? Are you raising your kids to become spiritual leaders one day?

• As a family, list the top ten priorities you want your family to concentrate on. Are spiritual priorities at the top of your list?

Ideas to put 'legs' to your children's prayers:

• Plan a special Saturday morning breakfast for your teenager and his friends. Silently pray for each friend who sits around your breakfast table.

TWO: JESUS PRAYED PRIVATELY

After His baptism, Jesus went into the wilderness alone to struggle in prayer for 40 days. (See Luke 4:1-13). He often went alone into the mountains to pray. He seemed to love the solitude. Jesus usually prayed privately unless it benefitted His listeners. For instance:In John 17, Jesus prayed aloud so that His disciples would hear His prayer for them. In Mark 6, Jesus prayed publicly as He gave thanks to God and broke bread for the 5000 hungry listeners. (Verse 41). In John 11, Jesus prayed out loud when He called dead Lazarus out of the tomb: "Father, I thank you that you have heard me," Jesus prayed loudly. "I know that you always hear me, *but I have said this for the benefit of the people standing here*, that they may believe that you sent me." (Verses 41-43 NIV, emphasis mine.) Then He called: "Lazarus come out!" He prayed out loud for the benefit of the people there.

"Do not be like the hypocrites standing in the synagogues and on the street corners to be seen by men," Jesus said. "Go to your room, close the door, and pray to your Father, who is unseen," (Matthew 6:5-6 NIV).

I believe we each need a private place to pray. And we need to have special times each day to go there alone to pray. I have a small room with a comfortable blue recliner. Next to it, I keep my Bible, pen and paper, some Christian commentaries and books. I also keep a set of Old and New Testament audio tapes and a tape player close by. At night if I am too tired to read, I lie back, close my eyes, sip hot peppermint tea, and listen to God's Word. My chair purposely faces the east window so that I can see the sun "rise" during my early morning prayer time. Alyce and Christian also have their own special spots where they go to pray privately. It's important that we teach our children that they can pray privately to God, that they can pour out their little hearts to Him, and, in confidence, know that He will always keep their secrets. Teenagers must know that they can talk with God even when it seems they can't talk with anyone else.

Buy a set of Old and New Testament audio tapes. My children love audio tapes. Play them as your child gets dressed for the school day, or as he cuddles up in bed at night before he goes to sleep. Not only will he learn the wonderful Bible stories, and God's truths and promises, but audio tapes also help him learn how to pronounce some of the more difficult words, names, and places in the Bible. Tapes can help him memorize scripture verses as he listens to the them over and over. After he has listened to the entire Old and New Testament, start over again.

Find a special place for your child to have quiet personal prayer time. We don't have to have a special room for prayer. Any place will do. I know of one woman who has a "prayer bathroom." With three small children, it's the only place in the house where she can be assured of some privacy! I have another friend who has a "prayer car." She prays as she makes her long commute to and from the office each day.

Jesus once told His disciples: "Come with Me by yourselves to a quiet place and get some rest" (Mark 6:31 NIV). Psalm 46:10 advises: "Be still, and know that I am God." Since Jesus prayed mostly in stillness and restful privacy, let us provide our children with a bedroom or playroom or an outside garden or tree house where they can go to God privately in prayer. In doing so, we will teach our children about the beauty of solitude. Sweet solitude – teach your children to savor it. They will learn much about God in solitude.

"...Solitude and silence are for prayer," writes Henri Nouwen. "The Desert Fathers did not think of solitude as being alone, but as being alone with God. They did not think of silence as not speaking, but as listening to God. Solitude and silence are the context within which prayer is practiced."[26]

Society shuns solitude. They are afraid of it. They label it "loneliness" or "boredom." They fill their hours of solitude with noise and activity, like white mice running circles on stainless steel wheels.

"In a world that insists on vertitude, action, goals, and achievement," writes Marie Dawson, "drifting or pausing in life is an unspeakable crime. It flies in the face of our cultural admonition to keep moving at all cost, to constantly 'do' and never 'be.'"[27]

For the Christian, however, "drifting," "pausing," and grasping solitude is to be sought and cherished. To spend time with God, to think, pray, meditate on the special relationship between the Shepherd and His sheep, we need time, quiet, and solitude. Solitude is so vital to the one who prays. "...Few will ever deliberately seek solitude. Many are afraid to be alone with their thoughts. They are intimidated by the idea of spending several hours in stillness, allowing God's Spirit time to speak to them."[28]

"Silence is required for deep change to occur. Once we are silent, it is possible for us to look into God's eyes and discover His response....."[29] Share this secret of solitude with your child, and teach her to pray trustingly and privately with Jesus, her faithful Shepherd. Have family prayer times that are listening times. Hold hands, bow heads, close eyes, and just be still before God. Encourage your children to spend time alone with God each day in their rooms. The more time we spend in solitude, the more precious solitude becomes.

We must teach our children to pray because:

• Prayer and silence "is required for deep change to occur. Once we are silent, it is possible for us to look into God's eyes and discover His response..."

Suggestions for teaching your child to pray:

• Pray for people in your church who are unemployed. Alert them to suitable jobs in your community.

• "Pray through Proverbs. As you come to verses that relate to your life, rephrase the verses into a prayer. For example, 'Lord, help me to not be enticed by sinners. Keep me from walking in the way with them'" (Proverbs 1:10, 15). (Quoted from Rebecca Livermore, "Raising Wise Disciples," *Discipleship Journal*, Issue 91, Jan/Feb. 1996), p. 83.)

• Study God's prayer promises: Philippians 4:6; Matthew 7:7; James 5:16; James 1:5-7; Luke 18:1-8; Psalm 66; 1 John 3:22.

During your devotional time as a family:

• As a family, save some money to sponsor a child. Send your money to an organization like World Vision, Compassion International, Tear Fund, etc. On her own, my daughter once used her allowance to sponsor a child in the Dominican Republic.

• On snowy days, when you can't attend church because of icy, unsafe streets, plan a family church service. Appoint a "preacher," a "song leader," a "scripture reader," etc., and worship God in your "home-church." If your neighbors are also stranded and can't go to church, invite them to join you.

• Reward your kids for memorizing all the books of the Bible. (Setting music to them makes them easier to learn!)

Ideas to put 'legs' to your children's prayers:

• Invite visiting missionaries to eat or stay with you. Your children will enjoy and learn from their stories. They can understand how God is at work in the world through the words of missionaries.

THREE: JESUS PRAYED SIMPLY

"One day Jesus was praying in a certain place. When He finished, one of His disciples said to Him, 'Lord, teach us to pray...'" (Luke 11:1 NIV).

In response, He gave them thirty-four simple words to pray: "Father, hallowed be your name, Your kingdom come. Give us each day our daily bread. Forgive us our sins, for we also forgive everyone who sins against us, and lead us not into temptation." (Luke 11: 2-4 NIV).

Just thirty-four words. That's all! It's a prayer that can be prayed in nine seconds.

Jesus also warned His disciples about making a show of "lengthy prayers" like the teachers of the law in their long robe-wearing, front pew-grabbing and lengthy-praying ways. Jesus strongly advises: "...When you pray, do not keep on babbling like pagans, for they think they will be heard because of their *many words*." He adds: "Do not be like them, for your Father knows what you need before you ask Him" (Matthew 6:7-8 NIV, emphasis mine).

Teach children that prayer is simply "talking with God and listening to God." We can talk with God using brief, everyday words. Prayer doesn't need fancy words. (Some prayer needs no words at all!) "When thou prayest," wrote John Bunyan, ..."rather let thy heart be without words, than thy words without heart." (John Bunyan, quoted from Warren Wiersbe, *Real Worship*, Nashville, TN: Oliver Nelson, 1986, p. 103.) Jesus doesn't expect elaborate volumes. Many a mature Christian has been wheeled into life-threatening surgery with these words on his lips: "Now I lay me down to sleep. I pray the Lord my soul to keep. If I should die before I wake, I pray the Lord my soul to take."

How can we teach our children to pray simply? Let us start by teaching them simple formula prayers. When my children were small, we prayed this "formula" prayer before meals: "God is great, God is good. Let us thank Him for our food." Hungry young children often grow restless with pre-supper "prayer tomes." Before bed, we prayed the simple formula prayer: "Now I lay me down to sleep...." They easily memorized these simple prayers, and they felt special that they could pray them with the family.

In 1652, H. Jessey (who simply describes himself as "a servant of Jesus Christ,") wrote this simple catechism for "Babes," or "Little Ones" for "all parents, schoolmasters, or others...that are to train up young weaned children, and need direction; the leader into all truth direct you." He writes: "*In the morning give thanks and pray*. Blessed be God that gave me sleep; and makes me see, and hear, and speak: God Almighty bless me, and keep me from ill all this day, for Jesus Christ's sake. Amen."

"*Before meat*. Blessed be God that gives me meat. God Almighty bless me and my meat. Amen."

"*After meat.* Blessed be God that gives me meat. God Almighty bless me and my meat. Amen."

"*At going to bed*. Blessed be God, that kept me from ill this day. God Almighty bless me, and give me sleep, and keep me from ill this night, for Jesus Christ sake. Amen."[30]

Pray sentence prayers. One or two sentences each will involve the family members in the prayer, and will also stress that prayer can be simple, not complicated. As children grow, so do their prayers. But prayer need not ever grow beyond simplicity. Mark Twain once pointed out to his many-syllabled friends: "Why use the word 'metropolis' when you can use the word 'city'?" Let us teach our children that simple words are often more effective than "many words."

Jesus prayed simply. We can too.

We must teach our children to pray because:
• They need to thank God for His bountiful, faithful blessings to them.
Suggestions for teaching your child to pray:
• Teach your child to pray brief, simple prayers.

- Pray together the prayer found in Luke 11: 2-4.
- Arrange for your children to learn sign language. Encourage them to then "sign" their prayers to God.

During your devotional time as a family:

- Encourage your children to invite their friends over for a backyard Bible study. Keep the study simple and serve refreshments.
- When you teach your child one of life's many lessons during family devotions, be careful to never sound as if you are lecturing her.
- Have a family "treasure" search. Read through the book of Proverbs and write down the "treasures" you find for future use and instruction.

Ideas to put 'legs' to your children's prayers:

- Plan to hold a "free car wash" and wash your neighbors' cars. Pray for your neighbors and community as you wash the various cars.

PRAY

FOUR: JESUS PRAYED BOLDLY

Jesus prayed with confidence that His Father heard His prayers and would answer them. We need to assure our children that God understands what they are going through, their frustrations, their hurts, their doubts, their temptations. Hebrews 4:15-16 tells us: "For we do not have a high priest who is unable to sympathize with our weaknesses, but we have one who has been tempted in every way, just as we are – yet was without sin. *Let us then approach the throne of grace with confidence (or boldly),* so that we may receive mercy and find grace to help us in our time of need."

In speaking of Elijah, James 5:16 tells us: "The prayer of a righteous man is *powerful and effective."* Remember, at the tomb of Lazarus, Jesus prayed: "Father, I thank you that you have heard me. I know that you *always* hear me." We can teach our children that they can pray *boldly* to the Father. They can pray with *confidence*. And that God will hear their prayers. But...while we teach them to approach God's throne boldly, we must also teach them that that does NOT mean, of course, that we can address God like He's some kind of "ecclesiastical bell-boy"! Praying with confidence does not mean that God jumps to answer our prayer with an instant and automatic "yes."

"Although hundreds of Scriptures tell us that God hears and answers prayer, it is important to acknowledge what most of us have already observed – that He does not do everything we ask in the manner that we would desire. Years may pass before we see the fulfillment of His purposes. There are other occasions when He says 'no,' or 'wait.' And let's be honest, there are times when He says nothing at all..."[31]

While we can approach God with boldness, we must teach our children that boldness must have the necessary boundaries of respect and reverence. The writer of Hebrews tells us that Jesus' prayers were heard "because of His reverent submission" (Hebrews 5:7b NIV). In the Garden before His arrest and death, Jesus prayed in submission to the Father: "Father, if You are willing, take this cup from me; yet not My will, but Yours be done" (Luke 22:42 NIV). Reverent submission means we approach God with a healthy sense of fear. Psalm 145 tells us: "The Lord is near to all who call on Him, to all who call on Him in truth. He fulfills the desires *of those who fear him*; He hears their cry and saves them" (verses 18-19 NIV, emphasis mine). When we help our children set boundaries of respect and reverence, they can then comfortably approach God with boldness and confidence. Without these boundaries, they might be inclined to snap their fingers and selfishly expect God to jump to answer them. Without proper boundaries, prayer won't be very meaningful to them.

My good friend, author and teacher T.W. Hunt, begins his day in an attitude and posture of Christlike submission. "Each morning when I prepare to pray," says Dr. Hunt, "I begin by kneeling. The act of kneeling is a conscious indication of submitting. Then before anything else, I spend several minutes meditating on the attributes of God... I want to be sure my heart senses *fear and reverence* before I proceed." Then he adds: "Any Christian can perform this deliberate act of submission. It also puts my prayer requests into the context of holiness and power."[32]

Dr. Hunt brings up an important point about prayer. Be careful about your posture during family prayer. My grandfather would ask his family to kneel in prayer. We knelt and prayed in the family room as an act of reverent submission. While reading from the Scriptures, you might ask your family to stand. We stand when we greet important people. Americans stand when we pledge our allegiance to the flag, we stand when we want to give due authority to others. Standing for Scripture readings shows children that God's Word has ultimate authority and that we should treasure it and obey it. My friends in Switzerland had special prayer stools made for each family member.

165

Like footstools, they offered a place to sit, and with one's legs tucked under the stool, they also offered a posture of kneeling. We bow our heads as a symbol of reverence toward God. We close our eyes to concentrate on His holiness. Let us teach our children about reverent "body language." Make submissive posture a part of your family devotional times.

We must teach our children to pray because:

• The prayer of a righteous man [woman or child] is *powerful and effective*.

Suggestions for teaching your child to pray:

• Plan to do something special for your grandparents. Remember to keep them always in your prayers.

• Ask your child to write down five ways intercessory prayers can make a difference in someone's life.

• Encourage your children to pray for those who are in drug rehab centers. Explain about drug addiction. If possible, let them talk with a teen or adult who can warn them about the evils of drug use.

During your devotional time as a family:

• Plan to have your next family devotional time at a favorite restaurant. (You might want to choose a quiet one!)

• Explain to your children the meaning of "evangelism." Ask your children to make a list of people they would like to talk to about Jesus. Help them make these contacts during the week.

• Study together the disciples Jesus chose to minister

with him. Find books on each disciple at your church library. Help your children to discover their strengths and their weaknesses. Ask each child in the family to choose his favorite disciple and to explain why.

Ideas to put 'legs' to your children's prayers:

• On a hot day, help your children set up a LemonAid stand in the front yard, and give free cold drinks to the neighborhood's children. If opportunity allows, encourage your kids to tell their "customers" about Jesus.

FIVE: JESUS PRAYED PASSIONATELY

The word "passion" means "to suffer." Passion is an "intense, driving emotion." Luke 22 records Jesus' greatest prayer of passion.

"Jesus went out as usual to the Mount of Olives, and His disciples followed Him...He withdrew about a stone's throw beyond them, knelt down and prayed" (Luke 22:39-41 NIV).

Matthew adds that "He began to be sorrowful and troubled. 'My soul is overwhelmed with sorrow to the point of death,' Jesus told them" (Matthew 26:38 NIV). Jesus asked the disciples to "stay here and keep watch with me." Matthew also tells us that "He fell with His face to the ground and prayed..." (Matthew 26:39 NIV).

Mark writes that Jesus was "deeply distressed" (Mark 14:33 NIV). But Luke adds: "And being in anguish, He prayed more earnestly, and His sweat was like drops of blood falling to the ground" (Luke 22:44).

Luke was a physician. When he heard the incident recounted, he would have noted Jesus' physical condition as well as the drops of blood falling to the ground.[33]

Were the "drops of blood" simply a figure of speech? I don't think so.

James Dobson writes: Jesus "knew fully what the crucifixion meant. The emotional pressure was so intense that great drops of blood penetrated His skin. Medically speaking, that phenomenon is called 'hematidrosis,' and it occurs only in persons undergoing the most severe distress."[34]

Indeed, Jesus prayed with bleeding passion in that garden long ago, for He suffered sorrow, fear, abandonment, and desperation far more intense than you or I or our children will ever suffer.

"...I find it strangely comforting," writes Phillip Yancey, "that when Jesus faced pain he responded much as I do. He did not pray in the garden, 'Oh, Lord, I am so grateful that you have chosen me to suffer on your behalf. I rejoice in the privilege!' No, he experienced sorrow, fear, abandonment, and something approaching even desperation. Still, he endured because he knew that at the center of the universe lived his Father, a God of love he could trust regardless of how things appeared at the time."[35]

The writer of Hebrews tells us that "during the days of Jesus' life on earth, He offered up prayers and petitions 'with loud cries and tears' to the One who could save Him from death..." (Hebrews 5:7 NIV).

What does this say to us today? Teach your children to work hard at prayer, to concentrate totally when in the presence of God. "It is not good enough to 'half listen' to God. He demands my total concentration on what He is conveying to me. He knows that anything less will leave me half-hearted."[36]

Martin Luther's dog, Tolpel "watched with open mouth and motionless eyes, and Luther said: 'Oh if I could only pray the way this dog watches the food! All his thoughts are concentrated on the chuck of meat!'"[37]

Prayer is not just sweet thoughts directed at God. We must teach our children that prayer is total concentration and hard work. If Jesus felt the urgent need to pray with such suffering and passion, how much more do *we* need to pray with passion!

How can we teach our children to pray passionately? Often, during the day, I telephone my good friend and Sunday School teacher, Jan Alsabrook. At times she sounds exhausted. "Been scrubbing floors?" I often kid her. No, she has been praying, and that's often harder than scrubbing floors.

When Jan prays, especially when she prays for others – intercessory prayer – she often prays so intensely that it physically, emotionally, and mentally exhausts her.

"Intercession means that we rouse ourselves up to get the mind of Christ about the one for whom we pray," writes Oswald Chambers. "Get into the real work

171

of intercession, and remember it is a work, a work that taxes every power..."[38]

One day, while reading Paul's letter to the Colossians, Jan began to understand this "hard work of prayer."

Paul writes: "Epaphras, who is one of you and a servant of Christ Jesus, sends greetings. He is always *wrestling in prayer* for you, that you may stand firm in all the will of God, mature and fully assured," (Colossians 4:12 NIV, emphasis mine). At once Jan understood her exhaustion. Like Jacob, in the Old Testament, (see Genesis 32:22-32), she too "wrestles in prayer," and wrestling in prayer is hard, exhausting work. How can we teach our children to wrestle in prayer, to pray with passion? Let us teach our children to have a loving heart for the world's people, as Jan does. Jan daily reads about them and their prayer needs in a book titled *Operation World: A Day-to-Day Guide to Praying for the World* by Patrick Johnstone. Through this guide, she learns about the world's people, where they hurt, what they need. As she prays for the hurting and hungry, the helpless and spiritually-lost of this world, Jan places her hands on a globe. If she prays for people in Haiti, she places her hands on that portion of the Caribbean. If she prays for people in India, she places her hands over the continent of Asia.

Prayer is such a privilege! Prayer is such hard work! Placing our hands on the globe and praying for the world's hurting people teaches our children to work hard at prayer and to pray passionately. Children enjoy using their five senses. Touching a globe, seeing the country being prayed for, and hearing a parent read about those people and their needs, help children focus their prayers and pray more passionately for a lost, dark world.

We must teach our children to pray because:
• "Prayer is fundamental in the Kingdom of God. It is not an optional extra, nor is it a last resort when all other methods have failed. Prayerlessness is a sin (1 Samuel 12:23). *We do not just pray FOR the work, prayer IS the work*! Prayer lifts Christian activities from the realm of human effort to the divine. Someone made the statement 'when man works, MAN works; when man prays, GOD works.' Through prayer we become co-workers with the Lord God Almighty. We move from time into eternity, sharing the eternal counsels of God...."[39]

Suggestions for teaching your child to pray:
• Find a comfortable seat at the local mall. Ask your children to silently pray for the people who pass by them.
• If you and your children witness a car accident while commuting, stop talking and start praying out loud for the people who might be hurt. (If you are first on the scene, be sure to call the police and, if possible, help the victims.)

173

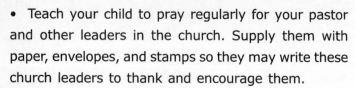

• Teach your child to pray regularly for your pastor and other leaders in the church. Supply them with paper, envelopes, and stamps so they may write these church leaders to thank and encourage them.

During your devotional time as a family:

• Make a family pact to stop complaining. Read together Philippians 2:14.

• Nickname your children after their favorite Bible characters. Ask them to tell you why that particular character is their favorite one.

• Use word pictures when you compliment your child. For instance: "Thank you, Christian, for helping me carry in the groceries. You are as strong as a lion." "Alyce, you are growing up to be as graceful as a swan."

Ideas to put 'legs' to your children's prayers:

• Help your children bake blueberry muffins for their Sunday school class.

PRAY

SIX: JESUS PRAYED CONSTANTLY

Paul writes in Thessalonians: "Be joyful always...*pray continually.* Give thanks in all circumstances" (Thessalonians 5:16-17, NIV, emphasis mine). The Psalmist writes "O Lord, the God who saves me, *day and night* I cry out before You," (Psalm 88:1 NIV, emphasis mine). David writes: "But I call to God, and the Lord saves me. *Evening, morning and noon* I cry out in distress, and He hears my voice," (See Psalm 55:16-17 NIV, emphasis mine). Jesus prayed before making important decisions. Before He chose His disciples, "Jesus went out to a mountainside to pray, and spent the night praying to God. When morning came, He called His disciples to Him and chose twelve of them" (Luke 6:12-13 NIV).

Jesus also prayed persistently. In the Garden, before His death, Jesus prayed *three times* that the "cup" be removed. (Paul also prayed *three times* that the "thorn" that he suffered from, be removed. In 1 Kings 18, the prophet Elijah prayed to God *seven times* before God sent rain to end a deadly drought. And, in Genesis 18, Abraham prayed with *nagging persistence* to God on behalf of Sodom and Gomorrah.) When we pray, Jesus tells us to ask, to seek, and *to persist* in prayer.

My friend, Sandy Luster, the mother of grown children, advises: "Make [prayer] a part of [your children's] day from morning to night. Teach them to converse with God throughout the day, to thank Him, to praise Him, to honor Him, to seek His guidance, to ask His forgiveness, to receive His unconditional love and protection."

Sandy has called on her children to ask the blessing at mealtime "since they could talk." "Occasionally," she adds, "we are reminded to 'thank Jesus' as [our two-year old granddaughter] stretches out her hands to be held."

When families pray together in this way, all throughout the day, prayer becomes a natural part of the day. Children will learn good prayer habits that will greatly enrich their lives and their relationship with God. "I am thankful that my parents taught me to pray daily," says Sandy. "...I never knew of a night when [my father] didn't kneel beside his bed for a long time in prayer."

When children grow up and leave home, prayer can continue to bind their hearts to home and family.

"It is exciting," says Sandy, "when our children, who are all away from home now, call just when I am missing them the most and say 'Mom, I need you to pray for me because I have an important exam coming up,' or, 'I am traveling this week,' or 'I am working on a big project at work....' Then I feel close to them again. I think after they are grown that, being in touch with one another through prayer, ministers as much to the mother as to the children!"

We must teach our children to pray because:
• The Apostle Paul writes in Thessalonians: "Be joyful always...*pray continually*. Give thanks in all circumstances" (1 Thessalonians 5:16-17).
Suggestions for teaching your child to pray:
How can we teach our children to pray constantly?
• In the morning, wake your child with a hot drink, and ask: "What's happening in your world today? What do we need to talk with God about?" Your child may tell you about an exam, or a bully, or a teacher who is ill, or a classmate who is rude. Encourage prayer to begin as soon as your child wakes.
• Before your child leaves for school have a prayer with her. Determine the length of the prayer by the amount of time you have. Mornings can be rushed around our house. "Lord, please protect Alyce as she travels to school. Help her to do her best. Bless her classmates and teachers, and help them all to know and love Jesus." A few sentences of prayer, a kiss on the forehead, and she will sense God's presence and your love as she faces a day at school.
• At lunchtime encourage your child to quietly bow

her head before she eats and ask God's blessing on her food. (I'm pretty sure that's still legal in the public school system!!!)

During your devotional time as a family:

• During school, especially before oral book reports and exams, tell your child to silently ask God to help him recall the information he studied, and to help him do his best work. (I often put a little note in Alyce's or Christian's back pack to remind them that I am praying for them while they are at school – especially on exam days!)

• After school, encourage your child to talk about his day. If possible, have a snack ready for him to eat. If he expresses concerns, stop then and pray about that concern.

• At supper time, remember to thank God as a family for the food on the table. If you find yourselves eating Whoppers in the car at the local Burger King, take a moment before you unwrap your burger to thank God for providing your supper. (How often I pause to thank God for fast food!)

Ideas to put 'legs' to your children's prayers:

• Before bedtime thank God for the day you just lived, for its blessings. Bedtime proves a good time to pray for other people, especially if you have constructed a "prayer wall" in your child's bedroom. Or, like Jan, you can use a globe to pray for the world's hurting people.

SEVEN: JESUS PRAYED LOVINGLY

One way to "pray lovingly" like Jesus, is to pray for others, what we call "intercessory prayer." Read the beautiful prayer Jesus prayed in John 17 to your children. How fortunate we are to have a prayer of this depth and description prayed in Jesus' own words! After reading this prayer, point out to your child that

- Jesus prayed for himself;
- Jesus prayed for His disciples;
- And Jesus prayed for you and your child.

Tell your child that Jesus still prays to the Father for him! Listen to Hebrews 7:25: "Therefore He is able to save completely those who come to God through Him, because *He always lives to intercede* for them." James 5:16 tells us to "pray for one another." This is the way we can show our love for God. When we pray for others, we show our love for our Savior, and we show our love for His sheep. No sweeter words can be said than those spoken to the Father on behalf of His child.

Whenever I close my eyes, I can see the slender form of my white-haired grandfather kneeling in prayer beside the family-room chair. It is one of my earliest and sweetest memories. So regularly did he pray for others, the chair's cloth arm was worn bare in the spot where he placed his hand. My grandparents spent most of their prayer time praying for others. As a skinny, pig-tailed girl, I remember my grandfather telling me that they called my name "everyday in prayer." I must tell you that as I grew up, married, had children, and dealt with a legion of decisions and pressures, I was always aware of, and comforted by, their loving petitions for me.

I now look back and realize that those were the dearest, most caring words Papa could ever say. Until his death in my thirty-sixth year, I always knew that no matter where in the world I was, no matter what situation I faced, no matter how I hurt or grieved, somewhere on a little farm in Rossville, Georgia, my grandparents were praying for me. It brought me a comfort and strength that nothing else could.

Jesus said: "Love the Lord your God with all your heart and with all your soul and with all your mind and with all your strength...And love your neighbor as yourself. There is no commandment greater than these," (Mark 12:30-31 RSV).

Intercessory prayer is the very heart of prayer, the prayer that not only blesses the one prayed for, but blesses the one who prays as well.

Austin Phelps writes: "We are never more like Christ than in prayers of intercession."[40] Jesus told Peter to "take care of My sheep; feed My lambs." (See John 21:15-19). What better way to take care of, to minister to, and to nourish, support, and sustain those whom Jesus loves, than to intercede for them in prayer? How important it is for us to teach our children to pray for others!

"Surely," writes Oswald Chambers, "the real business of our life as a saved soul is intercessory prayer," the "ministry of the interior."[41]

We must teach our children to pray because:
• Pray for others and you show your love for Christ and for His sheep. No sweeter words can be said than those spoken to the Father on behalf of His child.

Suggestions for teaching your child to pray:
• Read 1 Thessalonians 5:17 together. Talk about how your children can "pray with ceasing" or "pray continually."
• Pray now for the person your child will one day marry. Pray that his or her Christian parents are raising this young person to be spiritually-wise.
• If you have said unkind words to someone, plan a time to go to them and apologize.

During your devotional time as a family:
• Ask your children to encourage at least three friends this week.
• Together read Colossians 3:16 and discuss its meaning.

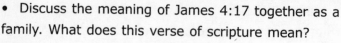
• Discuss the meaning of James 4:17 together as a family. What does this verse of scripture mean?

Ideas to put 'legs' to your children's prayers:

• Jesus prayed intimately, privately, simply, boldly, passionately, constantly, and He prayed lovingly for others. Jesus sets the perfect example of how we are to pray. And I believe it's the best way to teach our children to pray, for one day they will leave their childhood home and journey through life without us. Let us give them the gift of prayer before they leave us, for, through prayer, God will guide their steps and encourage their souls as they step into a world that is dark, hurting, and so desperately in need of their prayers.

SECTION FIVE

CREATIVE
WAYS TO PRAY

"FOR THE EYES OF THE LORD ARE ON
THE RIGHTEOUS AND HIS EARS ARE
ATTENTIVE TO THEIR PRAYER,"
I PETER 3:12

PRAY

MAMA'S FLOWER GARDEN

I can still feel the summer breeze blow through my braided pigtails as my grandmother and I walked among the many flowers in her backyard garden. So many years ago, yet the memory lives constantly in my mind. Early mornings and late afternoons, before and after the midday sun had brought its sweltering heat to the little Southern farm, Mama and I walked through her garden. It was our "prayer garden," and it was our favorite place to walk and pray. I can still see her frail, bent-over body as she touched the petals of each freshly-bloomed flower. Her eyes sparkled and shone with joy as she gazed upon each bud and bush. Hand in hand we walked till the morning sun rose or the evening sun set. Mama taught me much about prayer among her roses, lilies, tulips, iris, and crocus. Just to be in the midst of God's garden creation proved a powerful incentive to pray. But Mama encouraged me to pray for others as we strolled through the flowers. You see, throughout the long years of Mama's life, on every birthday, holiday, and anniversary, Mama's friends gave her rose bushes and flower bulbs. Spring after spring for decades, those bulbs and bushes faithfully burst into bloom. The garden of flowers quickly became a garden of friends. Hundreds of friends, some still living, some long since gone home. Mama took my little hand, and together we walked slowly and quietly from "friend" to "friend." It was a sacred time for me, a time of settled solitude. We stopped often to touch a treasured flower, and to voice a prayer for the person who had given Mama that beautiful bloom. Sometimes Mama stopped for an extra few seconds and looked intently, lovingly, at a favorite flower. That's when I noticed her lips moving in private silent prayer.

During our walks through her garden, she told me all about family and friends. I learned about my past ancestors, of brothers and sisters and mothers and fathers long ago departed, but everyday remembered and I also learned how to pray, and pray creatively. I saw that prayer need not be a rigid exercise. Prayer can be creative. And fun. As creative as Papa's patio stones. As fun as an early morning walk through a flower garden that still blooms, without fail, each spring in my memories.

Mama died years ago. Her backyard flowers died too. I guess they missed the touch of the loving gardener. Weeds now overrun the once flourishing gardens. A few of the grandchildren dug up some of

Mama's bulbs and planted them in their own gardens. Although I have none of Mama's bulbs, I have planted a flower garden in my own backyard. In ever budding flower, I see Mama's beautiful face. Early mornings and late afternoons, you'll find me there, in my garden, walking among the fragrant blooms, my hands reaching out to touch, my lips moving in silent prayer.

We must teach our children to pray because:
- "If you don't stand for something, you'll fall for anything." (Martin Luther King.) Prayer keeps our children standing for God.

Suggestions for teaching your child to pray:
- When a scripture verse speaks to you in a special way, write it down and share it with a friend.
- Pray for people suffering from AIDS.
- Pray for families who are faced with caring for someone with Alzheimer's Disease.

During your devotional time as a family:
- Visit a local art museum to study the religious art of famous painters. (Look out for special visiting displays)
- Be enthusiastic about church on Sunday. Talk about what will happen. Read together Psalm 122:1.
- Ask the chaplain of the local hospital for permission to visit child patients. Have your children pray for these patients before you go and after they leave.

Ideas to put 'legs' to your children's prayers:
- Water the plants of a neighbor going on vacation.

CREATIVE PRAYER

I believe that children can get so used to routine family prayers that they no longer hold their meaning. When we repeat the same words again and again, we often fail to hear them afresh and anew. While I advocate teaching young children the formula prayers, I also think that we should make prayer exciting, fun, and varied for our children. Children want to touch and see and discover. They want to use all five senses to learn about God and their world. There is no need that prayer ever become unmeaningful or boring.

I gained this insight years ago when my own young children became restless during a supper time prayer. As we always did, we sat around the table, heads bowed, hands folded, and eyes closed. We prayed together the formula prayer: "God is great; God is good. Let us thank Him for our food." Then Timothy began thanking God, as usual, for the supper set before us. After several minutes, a muffled giggle interrupted the prayer. With head still bowed, I opened one eye, aiming it directly at Christian, then a mischievous five-year-old. Tongue out, eyes crossed, fingers up his nose, he was midway through his favorite monster number. Alyce, at age three, tried hard to stifle her giggles. But big brother put on quite a show, and little sister proved an attentive audience.

We later reprimanded the children for their irreverent behavior. That's when we discovered our traditional family supper time prayer wasn't working anymore with the children. Lately, in fact, they seemed uninterested in praying at all. "God is great; God is good" had become too routine for them.

Alyce's giggle awoke us to the fact that we had stumbled into some sort of "prayer rut." Family prayer seemed too predictable for them. Maybe even boring.

We yearned for our children to develop a loving relationship with God through a fulfilling, joyful, and rich prayer life. We considered prayer a dialogue with a dear friend, a friend who loves us intensely, a friend intimately involved in our lives. We wanted prayer to become as spontaneous as smiling. We hoped to do something that would stimulate them to pray with excitement and eagerness. We knew we needed to make our family worship time more creative, more "child-friendly." But how?

Timothy and I put our brains together and we decided to make some changes. At first, the whole idea seemed overwhelming. So we decided to start small.

We must teach our children to pray because:

• As parents, we yearn for our children to develop a loving relationship with God through His Son, Jesus, through a fulfilling, joyful, and rich prayer life. We want our children to enjoy prayer as a dialogue with a dear friend, who loves them intensely and is intimately involved in their lives.

Suggestions for teaching your child to pray:

• Bake cookies for your mail carrier. Pray for him each day when he brings your mail.

• On snowy days, offer to help older neighbors shovel snow from their walkways. Pray for their physical safety during long winter months.

• Ask a child to read Psalm 141:3. Discuss how this scripture verse can help us to use careful and kind words when we speak to another person.

During your devotional time as a family:

• Talk with your children about speaking words of honesty. Read Hebrews 13:18 and talk about the meaning of honesty in everyday life.

• Take cupcakes to your local nursing home. (Ask permission before you go.)

• Tell your children the importance of keeping their promises. (Read Psalm 15:1,4).

Ideas to put 'legs' to your children's prayers:

• Take your child and her friends to the zoo. As you look at the animals, talk about God creating them.

PRAYERS THAT USE SENSES

Children pick up information through their five senses: seeing, hearing, tasting, touching, and smelling. When we ask a child to close his eyes, bow his head, fold his hands, and sit still, we are asking him to do the almost impossible! "Martin Luther is reported to have said that God gave us five senses with which to worship Him and that it would be sheer ingratitude for us to use less."[42]

How can we incorporate the five senses into a creative family prayer time? We can start with "open-eye" prayers.

On the first evening of our "prayer experiment," we asked Christian and Alyce to open their eyes during supper prayer. One by one, we took turns praying. Each voiced a prayer to God. Each one of us prayed a sentence or two. The next evening, they asked if we could pray that same way again. The experiment seemed to be working. For a change, *they were praying*, and *we were listening*. We learned something from our listening. We discovered that children expose their hearts when they pray. When Christian and Alyce prayed, we learned what lay heavy on their little hearts. These revealing prayers opened the door for many intimate talks later.

With supper time open-eye prayers, we can decorate the table with candles, flowers, or centerpieces to reflect God's love. A vase of flowers can show God's natural creation. A lit candle can reflect Jesus as Light in a dark world. Imagine what would come to little minds in open-eye prayers with family photos placed on the center of the supper table (Philippians 1:3). Or a toy lamb (John 10:14). Or a homemade loaf (Matthew 6:11; John 6:35). Or a piece of jewelry or baby cup that belonged to great-grandmother (Ephesians 6:18). Or the family Bible (Hebrews 4:12).

The open-eye, sentence prayers worked well for us at mealtimes, and at other times, too. We prayed sentence prayers as we commuted to and from preschool, soccer practice, and piano lessons. This was before cell phones, so we experienced few interruptions. Car prayers worked well then because we spent so much time commuting from place to place. They still work well today with our teenagers.

We must teach our children to pray because:
• Our children expose their hearts when they pray. They need a listening Friend who will always be there.

Suggestions for teaching your child to pray:

• Encourage someone who is struggling with a problem. Read Job 4:4 and discuss its meaning. Pray together for that person.

• Buy flowers and help an elderly neighbor plant them. Teach your children about each flower – God's beautiful creation of design and color. Pray daily for your elderly neighbor.

• Pray for missionaries on their birthdays. (Check with denominations to learn the name and date.)

• Read Galatians 5:22-23. Study each of the "gifts of the Spirit" so that small children will understand what they mean. Write them on a poster board, and post them in your kitchen.

During your devotional time as a family:

• Plan to do something nice for your pastor's wife.

• Write a letter to a family member or friend. In the letter, enclose one of the following: an individually wrapped tea bag; a stick of gum; a funny comic strip; a recipe; stickers; family photos

• Plan a date for a picnic/barbecue. Invite your neighbors. Ask each to bring a favorite meat and salad. Ask one of your children to pray before the meal.

Ideas to put 'legs' to your children's prayers:

• As a family, volunteer to work in the church nursery.

MUSIC, DRAMA AND CRAYONS

One evening Christian suggested: "Let's sing our prayer!" I blew the dust off the piano keys, and we incorporated music into our prayer time. We sang simple choruses, favorite old hymns, and put music to some Scripture verses. As the years went by, we added musical school instruments – clarinet, flute, and saxophone – to our prayer times. We also discovered that when we put God's Word to music, the children could more easily memorize the verses. In our home, scripture has been put to Bach's cantatas, Brahms' lullabies, "Motown," and even "rap." (As my friend, humorist Grady Nutt, used to say: "I sure hope God has a sense of humor. If He doesn't, I'm in big trouble!")

We have come to love drama prayers. One Christmas, the children surprised us with a uniquely creative way to pray. With friends and family as audience, Christian and Alyce draped themselves in bath towels and dramatized Mary and Joseph kneeling by the manger. That year, as we watched the birth of Jesus through a child's eyes, we gained a tender new insight into the wonder of Christmas. It was a special prayer offered to Jesus on His birthday.

During one family prayer time, we gave each child a new box of crayons and several sheets of fresh white paper. "Tonight let's draw our prayers," we suggested. Excited, they drew stick figures of Sunday School teachers, fellow preschool classmates, Grandmother, Grandfather, and Aunt Jill. We then prayed for each person captured in crayon. During the following months, many prayers emerged from these sheets of paper: the world's children dressed in colorful native costumes, missionaries holding hands and encircling the globe, faces of sick friends, and a crayon portrait of Billy Graham.

We must teach our children to pray because:
• God loves children's creative prayers. He gives them wonderful imaginations to worship Him.
Suggestions for teaching your child to pray:
• Choose a Bible verse to memorize. Have someone say the first word. Continue round with each person saying the next word until it is completed. Each time the verse is rehearsed, start with a different family member until each person has learned the verse. Play this game to learn the books of the Bible too! [43]
• Make a "happiness jar" for someone who is suffering from a terminal illness. For a month, during family

devotions, write brief notes (on colorful paper) to the ill patient. Tell them you are thinking about them, share a funny story, or draw a cute picture. Put the notes in the jar. When the jar is stuffed full of your individual notes, take it to the terminally ill person.

• Choose a wedding gift together for someone who is engaged to be married. Remember to pray for the couple on their wedding day.

During your devotional time as a family:

• Be careful not to discipline your children, especially teenagers, during family devotions. When problems arise, hold a special "family conference" to discuss them.

• Ask your child to do something special for her sister or brother that week.

• During your first winter's snow, bundle up and go outside with your children. Show them how different and unique each snowflake is as it falls from the sky. Tell them that God made them that way: one of a kind, unique and special.

Ideas to put 'legs' to your children's prayers:

• Make and send birthday cards to retired missionaries. Continue to pray that God will use them in His work even after they have officially retired from missionary service.

WALK PRAYERS AND PHOTO ALBUMS

One evening, when the telephone repeatedly interrupted our prayer time, we went out for a walk. While we walked, we asked the children a simple question: "What do you want to thank God for tonight?" Christian and Alyce's eyes sparkled with the majesty of autumn and the opportunity to thank God for His awesome creation. As we listened to the crunch of dry leaves beneath our feet, they thanked God for trees to climb, kittens to love, caterpillars to catch, and healthy legs to take "prayer walks." We waved to neighbors, patted pets, picked up interesting rocks, gazed at stars, and watched a glorious sunset. When we returned home, we read Psalm 24:1: "The earth is the Lord's, and everything in it, the world, and all who live in it...." My friend, Mary Jackson, suggests praying for each family in the neighborhood as you walk past their house.

My children loved to pray for others (James 5:16). But instead of just calling a name, I wanted them to

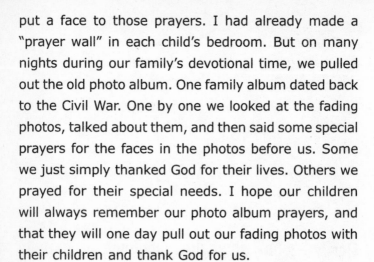

put a face to those prayers. I had already made a "prayer wall" in each child's bedroom. But on many nights during our family's devotional time, we pulled out the old photo album. One family album dated back to the Civil War. One by one we looked at the fading photos, talked about them, and then said some special prayers for the faces in the photos before us. Some we just simply thanked God for their lives. Others we prayed for their special needs. I hope our children will always remember our photo album prayers, and that they will one day pull out our fading photos with their children and thank God for us.

We must teach our children to pray because:
• Your neighborhood needs your children's prayers.
Suggestions for teaching your child to pray:
• Read the same Bible verses from several different Bible translations.
• As a family, adopt a college student in your church who is far away from home. Invite her for meals, Bible study, shopping trips to the mall, holiday celebrations, etc. Be her family during her college years.
• Invite a single mom to dinner. Ask if you can help her babysit her child, wash her car, fix her plumbing, walk her dog, etc.
During your devotional time as a family:
• Using the letters of your child's name, make an acrostic. List their God-given qualities and good personality traits under the letters. For example:

C aring

H appy

R efreshing

I nteresting

S weet

T alented

I nsightful

A wesome

N ever-failing

A greeable

L ikeable

Y outhful

C ourageous

E nergetic

• If possible, offer your home to someone who lives out of town, who has a spouse or child in the hospital in your area. Pray with him or her about the patient. Offer transportation to and from the hospital. Visit the patient with him.

• Buy baby items, gift-wrap them, and donate them to new or expectant mothers at various crisis pregnancy organizations. Look through your telephone directory for the names of organizations that offer alternatives to abortion. Pray for new and expectant mothers.

Ideas to put 'legs' to your children's prayers:

• Contact an inner city pastor and offer to take children from one parent families in his church ice skating or bowling. Tell these children how much God loves them and how special they are.

FAMILY VACATION PRAYERS

During a family vacation one summer, I discovered that family vacations offer scores of opportunities to teach children to pray creatively. A walk on the shore or beneath a rainbow, lead naturally into our retelling the story of Noah, and thanking God that He keeps His promises (Genesis 9:1-17). A trip to the mountains gave us the opportunity to talk about life, death and heaven. As we walked through the woods and watched dying leaves fall from trees, we stopped to thank God for Jesus, the Cross, and eternal life. During a trip to Grandmother's one spring, we touched and smelled (and tasted) our way through my mother's tomato and cucumber garden. It lead to a conversation about the meaning of Easter – of seeds, birth, Christian growth in Christ, and Jesus' resurrection (John 11:25).

We learned that "prayer prompters," like autumn leaves, rainbows, and tomato gardens, are ordinary objects that help children (and adults) understand abstract principles. In other words, they are earthly examples with heavenly meanings. As we go about a busy day, these objects serve as reminders to stop, ponder, and pray.

As we've already seen, Jesus used this technique in His teaching. When He spoke to people who worried about lack of food, He pointed to the **birds of the air**, who didn't sow or reap, yet were all well fed (Matthew 6:26). When His audience grew concerned about not having clothes, He showed them the **lilies of the field**, whom God had clothed in more splendor than Solomon (Matthew 6:28). He used a **mustard seed** (Matthew 13:31), and a **pearl** (Matthew 13:45), to explain the kingdom of heaven. I would imagine that, long after Jesus' resurrection, His followers never again looked upon a bird or a lily, a seed or a pearl, without pausing and voicing a prayer to God. Jesus knew that everyday objects serve as powerful prompters that cause our hearts to kneel in prayer.

Prayer needn't be boring! We can incorporate prayer into every aspect of family life, morning, noon, night, and all times in-between. Families can create "prayer times" that fit no traditional mold. God has given us such a beautiful world filled with so many things that can be used to glorify Him. We can be as creative with prayer as our imaginations will allow us!

We must teach our children to pray because:
• God has given us such a beautiful world to live in, a world filled with so many things that can be used to

glorify Him. As human beings, we need to worship, and we need to worship our Father who gives us life.

Suggestions for teaching your child to pray:

• If you have small pets, let your children take them to a local nursing home. (Ask permission first.) Pray silently for the residents as you visit. Many elderly people love animals, but have little contact with them. Keep your pup on a leash. Don't take iguanas, lizards, snakes, frogs, or mice. Many elderly people don't want contact with these small "pets." (Wash the dog. Don't try to wash your cat!)

• Make crayon cards for prisoners. On each card, write why you love Jesus. Quote some favorite scripture verses. Ask your church to mail them for you.

• Plan a surprise birthday party for a Christian friend.

During your devotional time as a family:

• Study the birds in your area. Build a simple bird feeder, and fill with the kind of seed these birds enjoy. Tell your children often about God's wonderful creation of birds. Invite your friends to "birdwatch" with you.

• Plan an "insect-collecting" adventure for the family. Find and identify all types of insects, and watch them. Wonder at the rich, unique ways God created insects.

• Buy an ant farm, and marvel at these industrious creatures made by God. Read books from the library and study the life of an ant. Read Proverbs 6:6.

Ideas to put 'legs' to your children's prayers:

• Bake a birthday cake for a nursing home resident. Make it large enough to share with her friends.

PROMPTING SPONTANEOUS PRAYER

We can also use a child's five senses to prompt spontaneous prayer. A friend once told me her daughter had been afraid to sleep alone at night. So she bought a print of a beautiful angel with a flowing white gown and a kind face, and hung it on the wall by her daughter's bed. Then she told her daughter that she was never alone, that God's angels watched over her as she slept, and she didn't need to be afraid anymore. On a poster board she wrote these words from Psalm 91:11: "For He will command His angels concerning you to guard you in all your ways..." From then on, when the child wanted to hide under the covers in fear, she looked at the angel and the scripture verse and remembered her mother's words.

I wondered if the same technique might work to help prompt Christian and Alyce to pray, and to pray more spontaneously. I wanted each child to develop *the habit of prayer,* just as Jesus prayed when He lived on earth. One day, as I wandered through a

Christian book store, I noticed with new interest the many colorful posters they had for sale. There were pictures of biblical scenes and stories and a variety of playful kittens and puppies, as well as spaceships and nature scenes. Beneath the pictures, I found inspirational thoughts and scripture verses.

"Perfect," I thought. That afternoon, I presented the children with all sizes, types, pictures, and colors of posters. They had a great time taping them to their bedroom walls. Each night, when I tucked Alyce and Christian into their beds, we read the message on the posters and talked about their meanings. I left a night light on in each child's room so that, long after I had gone, Christian and Alyce could ponder the pictures and scripture on those posters. The posters stayed on their walls for years. They served as visible reminders of God and His love for them. They also proved to be a good Christian witness for the many little friends that came in and out of the children's bedrooms.

We must teach our children to pray because:

• Children need to develop *the habit of prayer*, just as Jesus prayed when He lived on earth. The more they pray, the more they will want to pray.

Suggestions for teaching your child to pray:

• Write these words from Psalm 91:11: "For He will command His angels concerning you to guard you in all your ways..." Put it in your child's room.

• If someone in your immediate family is sick, ask him to sit in the middle of the family circle. Place your hands on him and pray that God will make him well. Pray that God's will be done in the life of that person.

• Keep a list of family and friends' birthdays. At the beginning of each month, check your list for birthdays during that month. Make homemade cards to send them. Tell each one you are praying for them on their birthday. (Mail them early so they will receive them on their birthday.)

During your devotional time as a family:

• Brainstorm creative ways to help new mothers in your church or community. Volunteer to babysit, and allow them to take a break.

• Introduce your children to a handicapped person in your church. Let them get to know this person. Teach your young children this little song (sing it to the tune of "Jesus Loves the Little Children").

> "Jesus loves the little children,
> All the children in the world,
> Deaf and blind and crippled, too,
> God loves them like He loves you,
> Jesus loves the little children of the world."

• One evening take everything off the dinner table except the salt. Read Matthew 5:13-16. Paraphrase for younger children what this verse means. Sprinkle a dash of salt in each person's palm and ask them to taste it. Discuss how each person can be salt in the world in which they live.[44]

Ideas to put 'legs' to your children's prayers:

• As a family, reach out to a boy from a single parent

family in your church or community. Invite him to join you on family outings, especially ball games, fishing trips, trips to the mall, etc. Become his friend, and share your faith with him.

PRAY

HISTORICAL TEACHING TOOLS

By studying the lives, and especially the prayer lives, of historical figures, such as well-known missionaries, we can show our children how to pray, as well as, the power of prayer. Check out books from the community or church library on figures such as Lottie Moon, William Carey, David Brainerd, George Whitefield, John and Charles Wesley, Amy Carmichael, Mother Theresa, and many others.

Through their devout lives and words, let these Christian "giants" teach your children how to pray and live a life dedicated to God. There are literally hundreds of Bible "heroes" who can teach your children about God and His work in our world, past and present.

If time and money (and international relations) allow it, plan trips to other countries with your children. Allow history to live for them as they retrace the steps of favorite missionaries, or learn about historical events. A trip to Israel, for example, would be an excellent opportunity to walk in Jesus' footsteps, something like this would stay with them for the rest of their lives and make their Bibles take on new life. It is unfortunate that international incidents can make travel to countries like this dangerous, as well as difficult, but other places in the world can be just as thought-provoking. I'll never forget hearing of Christian's deep reaction when he visited Hiroshima in Japan with Timothy one summer, or about his trip to a German concentration camp. Alyce acquired a love for Bishop Thomas Cranmer, his *Book of Common Prayer*, and his other Christian writings, when she visited England for the first time.

Before the trip, visit the local library. Let your child study what he will see during his trip. Study the culture of the country, its people, its famous missionaries, its native religions, the customs, and the food the people eat. Also purchase a travel book with blank pages. During the trip encourage him to record his travels, experiences, impressions, thoughts, and questions.

Traveling with children opens wide doors to their small world. They will take new interest in world news reports. They will learn that people have skins of various color, strange customs, and different cultures. They can learn that God loves these people, even though they are different, and that Jesus died for each person. Traveling abroad helps us teach our children how we should daily pray for the world's people. It gives children insight into how missionaries have lived and worked. Before your trip, contact missionaries in your denomination that work in that country. Arrange to meet with them, if possible.

Do it as a gift to your children. Let your children hear their stories, learn about the people they minister to, and discover their prayer needs. Encourage correspondence with these missionaries when you return home. My children email and write letters to missionaries all over the world to find out special needs, and to tell them we are praying for them.

Even though traveling with kids is expensive, time-consuming, often downright frustrating and exhausting, it's one of the best ways to teach children about life, God, society, and prayer. What children gain from travel experiences far outweigh the time, energy, and money a trip abroad requires.

We must teach our children to pray because:
• Missionaries work hard, in strange, foreign lands. They desperately need our prayers. Praying for them will also enrich the prayer life of your children.

Suggestions for teaching your child to pray:
• Read about Christian "giants" as a family in the evenings and then discuss their devoted prayer lives.
• Have younger children draw interesting scenes from the historical figure's life, perhaps a scene picturing the figure at prayer.
• Make popsicle-stick puppets together, and have your children perform the character's life.

During your devotional time as a family:
• Study the country where a favorite missionary worked.

- Prepare a family dinner using the same foods the missionaries might have eaten with their native people.
- Tell your children stories of many other famous missionaries, and make these figures come alive for your children. Let them be your teaching tools.

Ideas to put 'legs' to your children's prayers:

- Follow these basic prayer steps, and encourage your children to pray for missionaries in these ways: Pray for the missionary's:

- personal relationship with God, that it will stay strong and intimate;

- health, that God will keep his body well;

- emotional needs, that God may keep him encouraged about his work with needy people;

- safety, that God will provide for him and his family, and protect them from harm;

- family relationships, that they will be kept strong and loving, open, honest, and praying together;

- ability to communicate the gospel of Jesus Christ to a lost and hurting world;

- effective ministry to the people God has chosen him to minister to;

- team relationships, that he may work well with other missionaries serving in his area of mission;

- country of service, that he may truly love the people to whom he ministers, and has a heart to lead them to the Lord.

SUNDAY TOYS

For centuries, parents have been finding unique and creative ways to teach their children about God and prayer. Had we been parents in Colonial times, Sundays might have been difficult days to have young children around. You see, during those times, Sundays meant dreary afternoons for children. They were forbidden to run, whistle, or play. A person could land in "stocks" in the public square just for laughing on the Lord's Day. To help relieve cranky and restless children, parents came up with an incredible idea – a teaching discovery. They made what they called "Sunday toys." Inspired by Biblical themes, Sunday toys not only gave children an opportunity to play, but they were teaching tools as well. On Sunday afternoons, parents gave their children music boxes that played Christian hymns, or a board game that demonstrated the rewards of virtue and the penalties for vice (they called this clever game "The Game of Christian Endeavor"). Some parents set up a "biblical museum" for their children. They collected tiny specimens of plants and minerals that were used in Biblical days and placed them in a little carved wooden box. One of the most popular "Sunday toys" was Noah's Ark. They began to appear in the seventeenth century. During long winter evenings, fathers carved tiny animals from wood – two of every kind, of course. They kept the animals in a boat-shaped carved toy chest. Presiding over the Ark was a hand-carved Noah – sometimes clothed in loincloth, and sometimes wearing a respectable bowler and topcoat.

Each Sunday toy ark contained a cavalcade of animals that was limited only by the carver's creativity. The only constant in these early teaching toys was the dove that signified the end of Noah's trial and the salvation of humanity through his and his family's faith. ("Sunday Toys," *Discovering America's Past*, Pleasantville, New York: *Reader's Digest*, 1993, p. 30.)

Recently, some creative toy manufacturers have once again picked up the idea of Sunday toys for children. Most Christian bookstores carry an assortment of dolls dressed like David and Goliath and others, board games about the Bible, and kneeling-praying dolls. These tools teach children about the Bible, its characters, its lessons, its promises. I think they are useful things to teach our children about God and about prayer. But I tend to like the old-fashioned way of providing "Sunday toys" for our children. Here are six great creative prayer ideas for "Sunday toys."

1. *Homemade Board Games*: Encourage your kids to make homemade board games. One Christmas, 8-year-old Alyce made a wonderful board game using a large poster board and brightly-colored markers. The whole family sat down to play it on Christmas Day. She even gathered little household items she gave as "prizes" for the winners. She had our family members moving miniature people around the board, and quoting Bible verses, hugging each other, and answering Bible trivia questions like "who did Cain marry?"!

2. *Bible Character Dolls*: With a few old dishtowels, naked-neglected-tossed-in-the-back-of-the-closet Barbie and Ken, turn into Abraham and Sarah or Mary and Joseph. Dress these dolls in Biblical garb, and they will come alive in your children's hands. They will also allow you to teach your children about the good points and downfalls of various Biblical characters.

3. *A Bible Herb Garden*: Help your children plant various herbs, that were grown in Bible days, in their own window box or backyard. Most herbs are easy to grow. As the herbs mature, study together how Biblical people used them. Your children can touch the herbs, smell them, and even use them in some favorite recipes. (For instance: *Cinnamon* was used for perfumery (Proverbs 7:17; Revelation 18:13). *Galbanum*, a relative of *parsley*, was burned as incense (Exodus 30:34). *White marjoram*, related to the *mint*,

was used in Tabernacle ceremonies (Exodus 12:22). *Cummin* and *dill*, related to the parsley family, was a common culinary herb (Isaiah 28:25-27; Matthew 23:23). Jewish leaders tithed *mint*, a popular seasoning herb (Luke 11:42). Jesus referred to *mustard* for having small seeds which grow into a tree (Matthew 13:31-32).

4. *Plants and flowers.* Teach your children the plants and flowers people in Biblical days used. For instance: Did you know that the *Aloe vera* plant was used as a medicine (John 19:39) in ancient times, too? And consider these flowers (and read to your children these scripture verses): *Lilies*: (Matthew 6:28: "And why do you worry about clothes? See how the *lilies* of the field grow. They do not labor or spin" NIV.) *Roses*: (Song of Solomon 2:1: "I am a *rose* of Sharon, a lily of the valleys" NIV.) *Crocus*: (Isaiah 35:1-2a: "The desert and the parched land will be glad; the wilderness will rejoice and blossom. Like the *crocus*, it will burst into bloom...." NIV.) The lily, rose, and crocus are common plants we can purchase at any garden store. Other Biblical plants, such as the "papyrus sedge," "reed mace," and the "christthorn" can be studied and then drawn with crayons to make a fine paper flower garden.

5. *A Biblical Sunday Dinner*: While I personally consider cooking as work – hard work! (the motto around my house is: "where there's smoke there's supper!), children consider cooking as play. You can

make a "Sunday toy" out of "Sunday dinner." Teach your children about the grains, fruits, nuts, and vegetables people cooked and ate in Biblical times. Let them help you plan and prepare a Biblical Sunday dinner. Be sure to include some of the following: *Wheat* (Genesis 41:49; Genesis 47:24); *barley* (the poor man's wheat—2 Kings 4:42; John 6:9; Exodus 9:31,32; I Kings 4:28; Ruth 2:14); *grapes* (1 Samuel 30:12); *apples* (Song of Solomon 2:3,5;7:8); *almonds* (Genesis 43:11); *walnuts* (Song. of Solomon 6:11); *pistachio nuts* (Genesis 43:11); *onions, leeks, garlic, cucumbers, and melons* (Numbers 11:5; 2 Samuel 17:28; Daniel 1:12). Serve your children *chick peas* and then explain to them that these were the vegetables Daniel and his friends may have eaten in Babylon (Daniel 1:12). Make a big pot of *lentil* soup and then tell your children about how Jacob obtained Esau's birthright with this same soup (Genesis 25:29-34). If working in the kitchen with young children proves to be a safety hazard (more smoke!), then provide colorful magazines that advertise food. The children can cut the food pictures out of the magazines, glue them on board, and make a Biblical garden collage. Or you might till a small spot for a garden, buy some plants and seeds, and let your children grow their own Biblical vegetable garden.

6. *Popsicle-stick Puppets*: Encourage your children to act out Bible stories with cut-out paper puppets attached with tape to popsicle sticks or unsharpened

223

pencils. Timothy and I have spent many a delightful evening watching our children present Bible plays, and even some original plays. In their younger years, Christian and Alyce enjoyed hopping behind the couch with their handmade puppets and hand-written scripts. Not only did these plays prompt our kids to study the Bible, but it also encouraged them to write creatively. (Parents and children might want to work together to sew cloth puppets.)

7. (And, of course) *Noah's Ark*: Noah and his animals have once again come into fashion. Most bookstores carry the Ark menagerie in an assortment of colors, shapes and sizes. But even though Noah has gone "commercial," we can still make our own Noahs. Even young children can carve animals from bars of soap (using a case knife or children's scissors). Animals can be made from cardboard and paint, shaped from Play Dough, or twisted into forms using long balloons. (But be prepared to answer their first question: "Mommy, did Noah put dinosaurs on the Ark?")

MORE CREATIVE PRAYER IDEAS

Prayer can be as creative as your imagination permits! Here are some more creative ways to pray with your children: • *Pray with pen and paper*: My friend, mother and writer Cindy McCormick Martinusen, suggests: "Place a memo board in a high traffic area of your home, recording current family prayer requests. Parents and children can write their needs on the board." Also: "A bright, fun sticker on a lunchbox or notebook can remind children of the morning prayers. By weekly changing that sticker, the routine won't become dull or overlooked. Make it a game! Kids can find the secret coded message hidden in their backpacks or lunches and show Dad and Mom when they arrive home. Words like PAL (Pray At Lunch), DOM (Dad's Office Meeting), MMQ (Madelyn's Math Quiz) can be fun cues for children to remember prayer. With a touch of creativity, children can be reminded that prayers sent to heaven surround them throughout the day."[45]

• *Pray using maps:* Author Keith Wooden writes: "One family in our church has hung a world map on the living room wall. On the map are the locations of the missionaries they support and their pictures. The children in this family have opportunity literally to pray around the world for people whom they know personally because when the missionaries are home, they often visit here. I appreciate a family that will sacrifice a little decor for the impact and emphasis on spirituality can have on their children." He continues: "When I was a child a family down the street had a special bedroom set aside for visiting missionaries. It is amazing how much that concept affected my thinking, but I am even more amazed at how it influenced their children. Each of their children is now in full-time ministry for the Lord."[46]

• *Pray publicly in restaurants*: My friend, Rhonda Kelley, tells of two creative restaurant-praying incidents: "I went out to eat with my friend, Judi, and her very out-going five-year-old daughter, Sarah. Sarah wanted to ask the blessing. As she prayed, she got louder and louder. Her mother tried to quiet her but she loudly explained: 'I'm praying very loud so I can bless everybody's food'!" Another time, Rhonda went out to eat with her twin four-year-old nephews: "We blessed our food then someone sat down next to us and began eating without prayer. Loudly one of my nephews said, 'Aunt Rhonda, that lady didn't say her blessing'! Sheepishly, the lady bowed her head to bless her food. As we left, she thanked me saying, 'I haven't said a blessing in a long time.'"

• *Pray with bells, cymbals, tambourines, brass bowls struck with a knitting needle and drums*!: In her book on the life of Amy Carmichael, author Elisabeth Elliot writes: "Amy did not believe in keeping little children 'stretched out like a rubber band.' It was hard for them to sit still with nothing to do, especially if they were too young to know the words to hymns and prayers. So she gave them colored flags, and during the singing of certain songs, and to this day, they stand and wave their flags while older ones accompany the singing with maracas, bells, cymbals, tambourines, brass bowls struck with a knitting needle, and drums (big narrow-necked clay pots with a leather flap which is thumped over the mouth)."[47]

Whoever said that family prayer had to be a quiet experience! Always remember that "knowing God does not come through a program or a method. It is a relationship with a Person. It is an intimate love relationship with God...."[48]

We teach our children to pray, not because prayer in itself is a good thing – although it is, but that it strengthens our intimate love relationship with God.

There are many ways to pray. With children, and grandchildren. Be creative. Never allow it to become boring or too routine. Share your ideas with your pastor and with other families. Lookout for ways to make prayer interesting and exciting for your children.

SECTION SIX

DURING FAMILY DISTRESS

"MY MOST CHERISHED POSSESSION I
WISH I COULD LEAVE YOU IS MY FAITH
IN JESUS CHRIST, FOR WITH HIM AND
NOTHING ELSE YOU CAN BE HAPPY BUT
WITHOUT HIM AND WITH ALL ELSE
YOU'LL NEVER BE HAPPY."
(PATRICK HENRY, 1736-1799)

PRAY

A TIME TO CRY

I cried into the telephone when my friend, Helen, told me she had terminal lung cancer. My spiritual friend and mentor, Helen, had been as close as a mother to me for a decade. Born blind, Helen had "seen" the world through my eyes. Born sighted, I had discovered the world of insight through her eyes. We had loved and encouraged each other through sickness, surgery, disappointment and despair. I wondered how I could live without her. Tears were no stranger to me, however. Like the rest of humanity, I had cried before.

Only a few years earlier, on a hot August afternoon, I sat in the yellow porch swing and grieved the death of my beloved grandmother. My whole family had gathered at her funeral that day, some 300 miles away. But with the upcoming birth of my daughter only ten days away, I couldn't make the trip.

I had pulled close that day to the One who had also grieved the death of a loved one. My grandmother

231

had taught me over a lifetime to trust Jesus, especially in times of tears. Her loving words echoed in my ears: "Just trust Jesus, 'Nisey, with all your hurts."

So I did. I had been amazed at the rest and peace I found in God during the dark days that followed, when, even in my grief, life went on, and by Caesarian surgery my daughter, Alyce, was born.

On the days when death and new life seemed to touch fingers, God stayed close to me. In the midst of my fear and pain, He presented me a delightful surprise, my new daughter's tiny, wrinkled face. And through my tears, for the first time in weeks, I smiled.

On a dark and rainy day, one week after Helen's death, my friend, Terry, and I drove to Helen's home to visit her blind, grieving, husband. We were grieving deeply, too. I talked about the weather, about everything I could think of to hold back tears.

During Helen's ten-month battle with cancer, I had watched her trust so deeply in Jesus. She knew he also had known the pain of approaching death. She turned to the Father for strength, just as Jesus had in His hour of great pain and fear. I saw God fill Helen with courage. I, too, had turned to God for strength. I had prayed continually for Helen, for her husband and loved ones, and for myself.

Missing her greatly, Terry and I once again turned down the narrow road that led to her house. I silently prayed for encouraging words to say to her husband. Before getting out of the car, however, for some reason

I glanced up to the dismal sky. And there, arched high in the heavens, as if great hands cradled Helen's small frame house, an unexpected surprise awaited Terry and me. A rainbow, full of beauty, bursting with color, shone through the dark clouds. We stopped and stared at the rainbow, and through our welling tears, for the first time in weeks, we smiled.

Ecclesiastes 3:4 reminds us that we will have times of laughter and times of tears. In the rainbow on that dark and cloudy day, as in my newborn daughter's delicate face, I saw the reflection of God's face, the One who delights in our laughter, the One who promises to help carry our heavy hurts, the One who gives us peace in our tears, and the One who teaches us how to smile...again.[49]

When our children face heart break, when they lose to death someone they dearly love, direct them to pray with all their heart, mind and strength. Let us, as Christian parents, help them to see the rainbows bursting with color in the death-darkened, dismal sky.

We must teach our children to pray because:
• Our children will never find joy and contentment in this life if they are estranged from their Creator. Prayer brings everlasting joy and deep contentment. It brings health back to a weary soul.
Suggestions for teaching your child to pray:
• Encourage them to pour out their hearts to God. Tell them God keeps His promises and their

confidences. Read together Ecclesiastes 3:4.

• Pray together as a family over specific problems that you face.

• Trust God, and pray to Him in the midst of overwhelming obstacles.

During your devotional time as a family:

• Discuss how worrying about problems is neither helpful nor wise.

• Explain to your children that God is bigger than any problem you might face.

• Pray always as a family for your family.

Ideas to put 'legs' to your children's prayers:

• After family devotions, eat ice cream together! Take a break from grieving and look for rainbows.

FINDING RELIEF

When Linda and her family experienced some serious and unexpected money problems, Linda sought relief from the pressure and worry through prayer.

"When I woke up in the night and couldn't sleep because of money worries, I would pray verses from the Bible," she said. "My favorite was Psalm 4:8 (NIV): 'I will lie down and sleep in peace, for you alone, O Lord, make me dwell in safety.'"

Linda would pray ten minutes or two hours in the quiet of the night. She prayed, using the Scriptures, until she felt the anxieties leave her and peaceful sleep return.

What a wonderful way to help our teenagers and grown children find relief from their many worries and pressures. We must help our children understand early in their prayer education that we never pray alone. The Holy Spirit prays with us. At times when we hurt too much to pray, the Holy Spirit talks to the Father for us.

I once heard someone say, "We can't trust God and worry at the same time." When we pray, we place our complete trust in the One who loves us and who promises us, "Come to me, all who labor and are heavy laden, and I will give you rest" (Matthew 11:28 NIV).

We must teach our children to pray because:
• God hears our children's prayers even if they are too distressed or embarrassed to tell us their problems. God answers their prayers and relieves their anxieties.

Suggestions for teaching your child to pray:
• Study scriptures that describe the Holy Spirit: Genesis 1:2; Job 33:4; Isaiah 11:2; Romans 8:2; Ephesians 1:13-14; 2 Timothy 1:7; Hebrews 9:14.
• Ask the Holy Spirit to intercede for you as you pray to the Father.
• Trust the work of the Holy Spirit, do not grieve Him.

During your devotional time as a family:
• Ask your children to write down particularly meaningful and comforting scripture verses on an index card to post during the week.
• Look up the word "advocate" in a dictionary. What does it mean? How is the Holy Spirit our "advocate"?
• For deeper study into the role of the Holy Spirit, read what Jesus had to say in John 14-16.

Ideas to put 'legs' to your children's prayers:
• Volunteer your time to help with church youth camping trips, white water rafting, and other edifying youth activities.

PRAYER CAN CAUSE MIRACLES!

Something went wrong when Jan, the mother of two young children, went to the hospital for a simple knee surgery. A blood clot lodged in Jan's lung. In her weakened condition, doctors couldn't remove it, and gave her only a ten percent chance to live.

"I prayed all through that time," remembers her mother Florence. "Our friends and family and neighbors were praying for Jan day and night."

Amazingly, within three days Jan had become strong enough to stand the needed surgery. Doctors were able to remove the blood clot, but then gave Jan only a fifty percent chance of survival.

Florence and her friends continued to pray for a miracle of healing. One of Florence's friends later told her, "I prayed harder for Jan than I have ever prayed in my life."

And the healing came. Not overnight, but still it came. With the odds stacked against her, Jan fully recovered.

"I never once doubted that she'd pull through it," Florence admits. "I just knew with that many people praying for her, she would get well."

Can we expect a miracle when we pray? I believe we can if God chooses to work that way in our lives. Prayer is built on a genuine, loving relationship with God through His Son, Jesus Christ. God hears our petitions, dearly loves us, and truly wants what's best for us and our children. Mark 11:24 (NIV) gives us a promise about prayer. "Whatever you ask for in prayer, believe that you have received it, and it will be yours." This is a verse we must teach our children. When believers pray, miracles can and often do happen.

Prayer is one of the gifts we receive from God when we believe in and respond to His Son, Jesus. Prayer is God's open door to us. When we step through the door, we can experience intimate communion and relationship with our Heavenly Father.

We must tell our children that when we pray, we do not pray alone. For when we pray, we reach out and join the hands and hearts of believers who, down through the centuries, have also stepped through the open door and have had their everyday lives renewed and transformed through the power and promise of prayer. Truly, remarkable things happen when believers pray!

We must teach our children to pray because:
- Even though God often chooses not to work in

supernatural ways, He can answer our prayers with miracles.

Suggestions for teaching your child to pray:

• On an index card, write down the word "parakletos." This is the word Jesus uses for the Holy Spirit. Discuss what it means: "helper," "counselor," "comforter." Talk about how the Holy Spirit helps us when we pray.

• Describe a time when you felt helped by the Holy Spirit.

• Write a letter to God and thank Him for the gift of His Holy Spirit.

During your devotional time as a family:

• Answer this question: What is the difference between a "Spirit-controlled life" and a "flesh-controlled life"? (Read Romans 8:5-14 for the answer.)

• Ask an older child to read Matthew 12:31. Talk together about its meaning.

• Read Jesus' words about the Holy Spirit in Mark 3:29. What does He say?

Ideas to put 'legs' to your children's prayers:

• Go camping as a family. Build a camp fire, roast marshmallows, drink hot chocolate, and pray together for other campers around you.

HURRICANE HUGO

When my friend Jackie heard that Hurricane Hugo would hit her Charleston, South Carolina, home, she felt great fear. Expecting her first child within three weeks, she feared for their safety. She also was afraid she would have no home for her newborn child. On Wednesday night, Jackie and her husband quickly packed and left the city.

The next day, Hugo devastated Charleston. Jackie later returned to find their town house still standing, but the furniture and baby gifts were floating in water and sewage.

Few apartments were available in Charleston. Having no place to go, they continued to pray. With each prayer, each fear was relieved. They eventually found an apartment, and one week later Jackie gave birth to a healthy boy.

Prayer can combat the fears produced by great crises as well as the small daily fears we face. Teach your children to pray about their fears. In John 14:27

(NIV), Jesus tells us: "Peace I leave with you; my peace I give to you....Let not your hearts be troubled, neither let them be afraid." When we pray, we slip our hand into our Father's hand, and we find new strength to face our fears.

We must teach our children to pray because:

• God comforts us in our fear. Only God knows what is ahead for our children during their lifetimes. Christ gives us peace when we pray.

Suggestions for teaching your child to pray:

• How do we "grieve" the Holy Spirit? Read Isaiah 63:10; Acts 7:42-43, and Matthew 23:13,33. Discuss with your family members.

• Answer this question: When a person accepts Christ, is he immediately indwelt and sealed forever by the Holy Spirit? Ask a child to read Ephesians 1:13-14, John 14:16. Discuss as a family.

• Explain to your children what happened on the day of Pentecost (found in Acts 2:1-4).

During your devotional time as a family:

• As a family, follow local news stories of people in your community. Help those people who have lost their homes to fire; or have suffered flood damage, etc. Find out their needs, and while you keep them in your family's prayers, provide them with practical help too.

• Gather a box of new toiletries, gloves, warm scarves, socks, coats, blankets, etc., and, through your church, give it to the homeless in your city.

• Start a family clothes closet in your church. Donate good, clean clothing of all sizes. Mark the sizes on tags and pin to clothing. Volunteer to be in charge of clothing distribution.

Ideas to put 'legs' to your children's prayers:

• If you have internationals living in your community, or visiting your church, learn a second language so you can more easily communicate with them. Let them help you learn it, and help tutor them in English.

ACHING WITH LONELINESS

I felt lonely, sad, and depressed. My husband Timothy was out of the country. He would be gone three long weeks, with no phone communication. We were living in Switzerland, a breathtakingly beautiful country, but a very foreign land far away from family and friends. We lived in a tiny apartment building with fourteen other international families. There was one washing machine for all of us!

It seemed December had been filled with dark, dread, dead days, and today was no different. We hadn't seen the sun for months. Snowed in with two energetic toddlers, my problems loomed extra large. I carried yet another basket piled full with wet, dirty clothes down three flights of stairs to the laundry. A toddler hung onto each leg. When an ill-placed mirror on the basement wall caught my reflection, I took a look at my weary face, and I began to cry.

Hildegard, a German woman ten years my senior who lived on the top floor, was folding a pile of clean clothes. I did not know her well, but when she saw my tears, she put her arm around me and smiled.

"I think we needs a cup of tea," she said in broken English.

While her pet turtle entertained my children, Hildegard and I sat in her parlor and talked. I must admit I couldn't understand most of her Swiss/German attempt at English. And I'm pretty sure she understood very little of my American English with its southern twang. But we sipped warm tea and talked and listened and prayed together. And when I once again returned to the duties of motherhood and laundry, I felt better. I could face the day without tears.

Hildegard reached out to me that day with understanding and motherly tenderness. She knew the demands and exhaustion a single day could bring to the mother of young children, a mother who missed the tenderness of her own mother some 5000 miles away. She also reached out to me with practical help, temporarily offering me a quiet place, a listening ear, and a much-needed prayer. A simple gesture on her part, yet a moment of comfort and compassion I will always remember. She lent that same loving, listening ear to me often during the rest of our year in Switzerland. Hildegard became God's heart and God's hands to me. She reached out to me in the same ways Jesus reached out to the many women He met in His journey through life: With understanding, tenderness, compassion, practical help, prayer, and healing. And through my own pain, Hildegard taught me, by her unselfish example, how to reach out to other wounded people.

My children are now teenagers. Life as a woman, wife, and mother still brings its demands and exhaustion. And, yes, tears can come easily at times. How often I have wished that I could run upstairs to that little top-floor apartment in Ruschlikon, Switzerland, and share tea and prayer with Hildegard. But somewhere through the years, I lost touch with her. The last I heard, she had spent the last few years of her life in that same little apartment fighting terminal cancer.

But the compassion she evidenced still lives within me. It will always be part of me, as well as the loving touches from others that have also found a home in my heart. She may not have known it, but in her own tender way, Hildegard placed a trust in my life. She placed a responsibility on my shoulders. A welcomed responsibility. A God-given responsibility. For now, in my own life's journey, when I meet a wounded traveler, Hildegard's compassion reaches out from her own lips with warm gentle words... "I think we needs a cup of tea."[50]

Let us pray that we can be "Hildegards" to our children, spouse, and hurting neighbors. Pray that, throughout the lives of our children, they will find their own "Hildegards" to help them.

We must teach our children to pray because:

• Jesus reaches out to those who ask for His help. He also sends us praying friends.

Suggestions for teaching your child to pray:

• Pray together for the lonely elderly in your church and community.

• Pray for a sense of Christian community within your church.

• Ask your children to read Galatians 5:24-25, and then answer this question: "How are we supposed to live our Christian life?" Discuss.

During your devotional time as a family:

• Encourage your teenagers to volunteer to work at Christian summer camps.

• Encourage your children to volunteer to mow the grass, rake the leaves, or take out the trash for an elderly person in your neighborhood.

• Plan a family picnic. Take your blanket, food, and your Bibles. Have family devotions outside under a tree.

Ideas to put 'legs' to your children's prayers:

• Plan to start a special Sunday School class for single mothers. Teach it yourself, or find a capable teacher. Find out their needs, and work to meet them.

PRAY

THE FIRST PRAYER I EVER SAW!

It was the first prayer I ever *saw!* At least it was the first prayer I was ever aware of seeing. Let me tell you about it.

An angel in ski boots, Joseph and Mary in dishcloth robes, and a tiny shepherd still cuddling her bedtime bear, among others, stood waiting to walk to the straw-filled manger. Another Christmas pageant? Yes. But this was a pageant of hope, and one of the highlights of all my Christmases past.

Some five months before, my husband, preschoolers, and I had rented out our house, our car, and our cat, had stepped aboard a Boeing 747, and had flown to the Baptist Theological Seminary in Ruschlikon, Switzerland, for our teaching sabbatical year. I did not want to attend the children's Christmas pageant early that Christmas morning. I woke up with a sore throat. I felt miserable. I looked out the window and groaned when I saw a foot of new soft snow on the ground. The cold damp snow wouldn't help my throat, I moaned. I was in distress that early Sunday morning. But, in spite of sore throats and new snow, we bathed, dressed, and made our way to our old car, a car that had spent more time that year with the Swiss mechanic than with us.

Needless to say, the car wouldn't start. So, through a foot of snow, Timothy and I pulled by sled, one shepherd and one angel one mile to church.

I sat quietly in the pew of the small bilingual chapel located on the edge of the seminary campus and wished I was 5000 miles away celebrating Christmas with the rest of my family and friends.

As always, when I grumble the loudest and expect the least, the God who came one star-lit night came to me in a fresh and vivid way.

The children of the seminary's sixty international students would perform in the pageant. These children had fascinated me. They came from affluent as well as poor war-torn countries. They arrived all ages, shapes, sizes, and colors. All had left families, school, and friends to come to this foreign place.

The children gathered in the back of the church waiting to start. Vera, Leo, and Grada from Holland; Tobit from India; Emmanuel and Gift from Africa; Bromlyn and Fiona from Australia; Mecal from Sweden; Dragana from Yugoslavia; Christian and Alyce from the United States.

They waited quietly back there together, unaware they represented every continent of the world.

Then, one by one they walked down the church aisle, singing songs, grinning at their admiring parents, and speaking their memorized Swiss-German lines. By the end, each child had knelt at the manger and had offered his or her handmade present to the plastic doll who posed as the Baby Jesus.

Just another Christmas pageant, one of many performed around the world that day. It wasn't even the perfect pageant. A shepherd's costume slipped off, a wise man sat on his crown, and an angel forgot her line. True, I had seen more perfect Christmas pageants, but surprisingly, never before had I seen one more meaningful.

As I sat there and watched these children of all colors and all cultures speak a common language and walk hand-in-hand to kneel at the manger, I felt a strong stirring of hope. For each child brought his own unique gifts, and each walked in harmony with the child who walked next to him or her. For me these children gave the world a face. And whatever the color of that face, it was the face of a friend.

On this Christmas morning, they had joined together to honor the One who loved their uniqueness and who celebrated their unity. For the love of Christ had brought them together in their differences, and their differences no longer made a difference. They walked together, brother and sister, to bring us the message of love and peace – the message of Jesus Christ. It was a moment of unexpected hope that reached out on that cold and snowy Christmas morning and touched me deeply.

Our year in Switzerland came to an end the following August, and we flew home. Since then, I've tried to remember all the wonders of Switzerland – the mountains, the cathedrals, the museums. But no mountain, cathedral, or museum could in any way equal the wonder and beauty of the little angel in ski boots, Joseph and Mary in their dishcloth robes, and the tiny shepherd still cuddling her bedtime bear.[51]

We must teach our children to pray because:
• Prayer changes bad attitudes. God speaks to us through the prayers we *see.*
Suggestions for teaching your child to pray:
• Write prayer notes. When your family pray for someone in particular need, encourage your child to write a note to that person. It is good for the child and the recipient.
• Buy your child a notebook. Encourage him to record prayers when distressed and share them with the family.
• Encourage Christian sports. Team up your child with a good Christian coach. Encourage the coach to pray with the team members before and after games and practices. They will learn much more than just sports from a dedicated Christian coach.
During your devotional time as a family:
• Celebrate "rites-of-passage" occasions. Include

family prayer whenever you observe significant occasions of life, such as birthdays, weddings, funerals, moving to a new home, joining a new church, adding a new baby, or graduating from school.

• Teach your child to pray when away from home. (Parents have often told me of my children's prayers when visiting their homes. One mother told me that my son suggested that he and her child start a children's prayer chain! Let us teach our children to seek God's presence and to pray wherever they go.)

• Let your children hear you pray for them in these ways: Pray for their salvation (John 3:16); Pray that they will thirst after righteousness (Matthew 5:6); Pray that they will remain pure (Psalm 119:9; 1 Thessalonians 4:3). Pray that while they are in the world they will not become of the world (John 17:15).

Ideas to put 'legs' to your children's prayers:

• Pray through the newspaper. Reports of a missing child in another state or of a flood that destroys a city, can prompt your child to pray for a hurting humanity. By praying for those whom they do not know, children learn about the power of intercessory prayer. Clip the newspaper articles and post them in plain view in your home. This will remind your children to pray throughout the week.

SECTION SEVEN

HOLIDAY PRAYERS

"PEOPLE IN THIS WORLD ARE LOST AND
UNLOVED. HOLIDAYS MAKE LONELY
PEOPLE FEEL LONELIER. WHEN WE ASK
OUR CHILDREN TO PRAY FOR PEOPLE
DURING THE HOLIDAYS, THEY LEARN
COMPASSION, SYMPATHY, AND AWARENESS
OF THE WORLD'S NEEDS. THEY ALSO
LEARN TO LOVE PEOPLE WITH GOD'S
HEART AND GOD'S HANDS."
DENISE GEORGE

PRAY

NEW YEAR

• As a family, and individually, ask God to direct your steps in the New Year.

• Make a priority list.

• Ask God's forgiveness for all your mistakes during the past year.

• During family devotions, discuss the past year – its happy occasions, disappointments, its surprises, and its losses. Pray that God will bless your family in this New Year and keep you safe from accident and disease.

• List ways you and your family can reach out to love and help others around you, and around the world, in the New Year.

MARTIN LUTHER KING DAY

• Take the opportunity to focus on reconciliation between the races. Help your children to learn that "the human heart is everywhere the same, whether it beats under a black skin or a white one."[52] Help them to understand that God wants all hearts to give themselves to Him.

• Visit the church service of another race and culture.

- Pray for those who, throughout history, have been abused by society because of the color of their skin.
- If possible, take part in Martin Luther King Day celebrations in your community.
- If Martin Luther King Day is a new idea to your culture start a new tradition. Your local school may be interested in teaching classes about Martin Luther King and the other social and historical aspects of this time period. Volunteer to help supply material or information or perhaps help out or organize a school social to mark the event.

ST. VALENTINE'S DAY

- Make homemade Valentines with paper, crayons, glitter, and glue. Take or send these cards to your grandparents, friends, Sunday school teachers, pastor, youth leaders, etc.
- With your children, bake a heart-shaped cake. Attach a card to the cake. On the card write a scripture verse about God's love. Take to the local nursing home or to a sick or homebound friend.
- Have each family member name three reasons why he loves the other family members.
- Adopt a new family at church, and plan together a special Valentine's dinner at your home.
- On Valentine's Day, ask your teenager (or oldest child) to read 1 Corinthians 13.

EASTER

• Make Easter cards to send to patients in your local hospital. If there is an AIDS ward send the cards there or perhaps to children who are spending Easter in hospital instead of at home.

• During your Easter celebrations, read Easter hymn lyrics out loud and then sing the hymn.

• Have family devotions by candlelight at night during Easter week.

• During spring break, do something nice for a neighbor. For instance: help them tidy their garage.

• Take a pizza and soft drinks to your next Bible study class at church during Easter week.

• Change your Easter traditions. Plan a fun vacation together during your child's spring break.

• Be aware of "teachable moments" that pop up during family holidays. Take advantage of every holiday moment to teach your child something about God.

MOTHER'S DAY

When my son, Christian, was 10 years old, he wrote an article titled: "25 Ways to Say 'I Love You' to Mom on Mother's Day." Your children might enjoy using some of his suggestions on Mother's Day.

• Make her a "Happy Mother's Day" card and leave it on her nightstand.

• Watch baby sister so Mom can sleep a little bit later.

• Greet her when she wakes up with a loud "Happy Mother's Day, Mom!"

- Surprise her by feeding the guinea pigs and baby sister – all by yourself.
- Open the curtains and window blinds so Mom can wake up to sunshine.
- Make her some eggs for breakfast (just the way she likes them) and give her some toast to go with it.
- Write her a note that says, "I love you lots," and, "Jesus loves you, too."
- Pick up your dirty socks and put them in the dirty clothes basket.
- Wash your ears and get dressed for church before she tells you.
- Be nice to your sister – for as long as you can.
- Get the morning paper early so Mom can be the first one to read it...even the comics.
- When she comes downstairs after getting dressed tell her she looks pretty.
- Brush your teeth before Mom reminds you, and put the cap back on the toothpaste tube.
- Put on your new tight, yucky, Sunday shoes the first time she asks you. And don't fuss about them.
- Behave in church, and don't whisper or wiggle during the Mother's Day sermon.
- Don't tell anybody at church how old your mom is.
- Draw a picture of your mom – and make her look skinny.
- Don't make funny faces at your sister during lunch.
- Pick your mom a wild flower.
- Memorize her favorite Bible verse by heart.

- Smile at her at least three times that day.
- Take the frogs, rocks, and chewed chewing gum out of your pants pockets – before she has to.
- Offer to let her sleep with your favorite teddy bear.
- Sing her a lullaby, and before she goes to sleep say, "I love you, Mom."[53]

FATHER'S DAY

- Wash the car without being asked.
- Polish Dad's shoes for church.
- Make a Father's Day card for Dad. On the front draw a picture of Dad enjoying his favorite hobby.
- Serve Dad breakfast in bed.
- Go to both Sunday services as a family.
- Tell Dad 213 reasons why you love him, admire him, and appreciate him.

GRANDPARENT'S DAY

- Make cards and tell them why you love them.
- Pray a special prayer for your grandparents.
- Pray for people who no longer have grandparents.
- Thank God for godly grandparents.
- If possible, visit them on Grandparent's Day.
- Pray through grandmother's old photo albums.
- Take your grandfather fishing. If he catches any edible fish, offer to clean them and fry them.
- Share with your grandparents your favorite childhood memories.

HALLOWEEN

- Discourage your children from "trick or treating" on Halloween night. Instead, plan a party for their friends.
- Discuss how and why Christians should celebrate Halloween. Explain that they should not be involved with the evil practices associated with Halloween.
- If you do allow your children to go "trick or treating," go with them. Take them only to the houses of friends.
- Dress children in funny costumes, not scary ones.
- Help with the school festival. These are more popular as "trick or treating" becomes more dangerous.
- Carve a happy pumpkin not a scary one.
- Monitor the programs your children watch on television during Halloween week.
- Ask your pastor about Martin Luther and the Reformation. Use library books and study together what exciting event happened on October 31, 1517.
- If you live near a college or divinity school, ask if they will be sponsoring Reformation Lectures during October. Attend these lectures or buy the tapes.

THANKSGIVING DAY

- If your country doesn't celebrate Thanksgiving Day – start a new family tradition.
- Ask a city pastor if you can help his church prepare Thanksgiving dinner to feed the hungry.
- Before Thanksgiving Day, buy a bag of food and donate to an inner city church or homeless charity.
- Invite international students to Thanksgiving dinner.

- Decorate your house for Thanksgiving.
- Check out library books that tell about the first Thanksgiving Day, and read them together as a family.
- Stick this on a bathroom mirror: "Thanksgiving isn't a holiday. Thanksgiving is an attitude." (T.W. Hunt)
- Ask each family member to make a list of what he is most thankful for this Thanksgiving.
- Pray a prayer of Thanksgiving for all God's blessings. Before you eat Thanksgiving dinner, pray for those around the world who are hungry. Decide on ways you can help them.
- If possible, get together with your larger family.
- Contact by letter all those people you want to thank specifically for some kindness they gave to you.
- Thank by telephone or in person, the Christian who told you about God and lead you to belief in Christ.
- If your community holds an annual community Thanksgiving service, go as a family.
- Help your church family distribute food to needy families in your city.

CHRISTMAS

- Offer to help an elderly person in your neighborhood gift wrap her Christmas gifts.
- Buy and decorate a Christmas tree for someone who is elderly or ill.
- Help your neighbors carry out their used Christmas trees after the holidays.
- Bake loaves of fruit cake and give to your neighbors.

• Make special Christmas cards for people in the hospital. If possible, visit them.

• With several other families, go Christmas caroling in your neighborhood.

• Pray specific prayers during Christmas: "Dear Lord, please bring our whole family together safely for Christmas." "Jesus, please keep Aunt Hattie alert while she drives to our home." Steer your children away from praying general prayers: "God bless everybody this Christmas."

• Ask children to help you decorate your home for Christmas.

• Bake a special birthday cake to celebrate the day of Christ's birth. Let your younger children decorate it with icing and candles.

• Get your children involved in your church's Christmas play or pageant.

• Tell your children about the wonderful Christmas Day dinners long ago at your grandparents' home. Describe to them some of your favorite childhood Christmases.

• Using construction paper and colored pencils, let your younger children draw a Christmas Nativity Scene. Hang on your refrigerator.

• On Christmas morning, plan a special breakfast. Before you eat, ask your teenager to read the Christmas story (Luke 2:1-20).

• Check out books from your community or church library, and study the ways other cultures around the

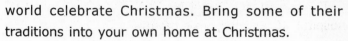

world celebrate Christmas. Bring some of their traditions into your own home at Christmas.

• As a family, take an elderly person to the mall, and help her shop for Christmas presents for her family.

• Shop for a handicapped person.

• Visit your library for a book that will teach you about Christian symbols and what they mean. Using styrofoam, glue, and glitter make ornaments for the Christmas tree in the shape of Christian symbols.

• Instead of giving store-bought gifts, make homemade gifts.

• Instead of giving Christmas gifts, send the money you would have spent to feed the world's hungry.

• Make a Christmas box for a missionary family. Include all those things they cannot buy in the foreign country where they serve.

NATIONAL HOLIDAYS

• During national holidays, display your flag. Or if you don't normally do this try and encourage the children to do something patriotic such as learning your national anthem or writing a letter to your head of state, president or prime minister.

• Pray for those who have fought for their country and who now suffer with disability. Pray for those who have lost family members to fighting. Thank God for those who have given their lives for their country.

• Study the lives of world leaders, particularly those who have been Christians. You will find that quite a

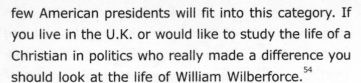

few American presidents will fit into this category. If you live in the U.K. or would like to study the life of a Christian in politics who really made a difference you should look at the life of William Wilberforce.[54]

• Pray with your children using examples from history: Children can learn much about prayer by studying the lives of Christian leaders. There are examples of praying Christians from both sides of the Atlantic and many other countries besides. If you live in America you could purchase a copy of Catherine Millard's *A Children's Companion Guide to America's History*, and read it together as a family. "With so many history books having purposely removed any reference to God and Christianity," she writes, "make sure you are teaching your children the truth!" As well as this look out for material about some well known Christians such as Andoniram Judson, George Mûller, Gladys Aylward and others. Christian Focus Publications has several publications in their Trailblazer and Lightkeepers series that would be suitable.[55] These real life stories all have examples of how Christians prayed and how God answered them.

• If you can try and visit places that are connected to real life Christian stories like this. In America you could visit many places connected to the founding fathers in Washington or Boston for example. In the United Kingdom there are museums which give information about David Livingstone, Dr. Barnardo, Mary Slessor, Wilfred Grenfell and others.[56] Do some research before you go on holiday and see if there are any places of interest in the locality that are connected to Christians past and present. You may find that there are monuments to local martyrs or famous local Christians. It is worth while contacting local churches before you visit for information.

BIRTHDAYS AND ANNIVERSARIES

• Surprise the birthday person with a cake and a handmade birthday card.

• Throw a surprise party, and invite the birthday person's friends.

• Pray for the person who was born on this day.

• Make a poster board for the birthday person. Have each guest sign his name, add some humorous advice, and pen their favorite scripture verse. Read the poster board at the party.

• Mark special anniversaries with special parties.

• Make every day an occasion to celebrate.

• For the adopted child, celebrate her birthday, and also her adoption day into your family.

• Tell the birthday girl or boy at least 500 things you love about them!

• If you have family members no longer living, thank God for each of them on their birthdays and special anniversaries. If possible, visit the cemetery where the family member's body is buried. Tell your children that even though "Mama's" and "Papa's" bodies are dead, because they are Christians they are very much alive with Christ right now in heaven. If allowed, take flowers and let your children put them on the graves.

SECTION EIGHT

FROM THE HEART

WHEN THOU PRAYEST,
RATHER LET THY HEART
BE WITHOUT WORDS
THAN THY WORDS
BE WITHOUT HEART.
JOHN BUNYAN

QUESTIONS AND ANSWERS

QUESTION: "Why should we pray together as a family? Why are family devotions so important?
ANSWER: Praying together as a family:
1. teaches children to worship God;
2. teaches children to pray;
3. teaches children the Bible;
4. teaches children moral values;
5. teaches children to love others;
6. bonds a family together and helps family members to more deeply communicate with each other.

Note: "A study by the national Family Institute found that the average parent spends 14.5 minutes a day communicating with each child. Of that time, 12.5 minutes are devoted to parental criticism or correction. A strong family cannot be built upon two minutes of communication per day. Positive and frequent communication helps to establish common family values which reinforce a family's sense of oneness."[57]

QUESTION: "How should we structure our prayer time together?"

ANSWER: Although much will depend on the ages of your children, try to include the following ideas into your family worship time:

1. Hold hands and pray together. Voice your concerns and desires to God. Family devotions bring family members together to talk to God and to better love each other. When we talk to God, we bring to Him our most heartfelt needs and wants. To express those things to God, as a family, joins a family in a deeper bond of communication and oneness.

2. Encourage your children to express themselves to God through prayer. In family prayer, encourage each member to participate fully in the devotional time together. Sentence prayers are a good way to include everyone.

3. Read the Bible together. Chose a book like Proverbs, and each day read several verses. Proverbs brings out special spiritual wisdom that parents can use to teach children moral values.

4. Encourage your children to memorize verses from the Bible. Allow them a time to quote learned verses during family devotions. Be generous with your praise. A young girl in my church recently memorized the book of James and presented it as a gift to her parents. What gift could be more appreciated?!

5. Reading stories from the Bible also teaches children how to live a Christian life, and opens up avenues for

family discussion. Introduce them to the fascinating Bible characters and talk about their lives. Bible personalities come alive when studied closely by the family.

QUESTION: "How else can I teach my children to reach out and love and pray for other people who are different from them?"

ANSWER: I believe God expects for us to reach out and love and nurture His people. We live in such a "me" society – a selfish world. I pray my children won't grow up to be "navel-gazers," self-centered adults who are interested only in their own lives. Jesus told His disciples: "My command is this: Love each other as I have loved you. Greater love has no one than this, that he lay down his life for his friends" (John 15:12-13 NIV). Jesus gave us the beautiful example of service to others when He bent down and washed the dirty feet of His disciples. (See John 13:1-17.) In that day, washing another's feet was a job that only the lowest of hired servants was required to do. Truly, if we love Jesus, we will love and serve His people. We teach our children to love others by teaching them to pray regularly for the needs of others. Intercessory prayer points our children to a hurting, suffering world, and gives them the heart of Jesus to reach out and help them.

Read to your children the wonderful story found in John 21. By the seashore, with 153 fish by their feet, the risen Jesus forgave Simon Peter for his earlier denial. (See John 18:15-18.) Jesus reinstated Peter with this question: "Simon son of John," Jesus asked, "do you truly love me more than these?" After Simon Peter affirmed his love for Jesus, Jesus gave him a simple command: "Feed my lambs," He told him, "...Take care of my sheep." (See John 21:15-19 NIV.) Explain to your children that Jesus gives each Christian the same simple command, the command to reach out to a hurting world with Christ's love and message. "Feed my lambs," Jesus tells us today. "Take care of my sheep."

QUESTION: "We are a busy family. We try to pray together every day, but we just can't always do it. What should we do?"

ANSWER: Pray together whenever you can. Make a genuine effort to have family devotions as often as possible. At least once a day is the ideal. Even a short family devotional time works better than no time at all. While we can strive for the ideal, we must be realistic. Moms and Dads travel these days; children have hours of homework in the evenings; unexpected guests or relatives often drop by; activities and emergencies can eat up family prayer time. Find a time that works best for your family. Have family devotions even when a member of the family is traveling or must miss it for some reason. And remember that prayer isn't just something we do, but who we are. We are a praying Christian family, and we live and breathe prayer all day, every day. Let us be careful to teach our children that, even in the chaos of a busy life, prayer is a priority in our family.

QUESTION: "When is the best time to start praying as a family?"

ANSWER: "Start very very young," writes Florence Lawrence, the mother of grown children and grandchildren. "Even the smallest child will imitate what you do. If they see you pray they will learn to. They like to say the blessing before they eat and say their prayers at bedtime with your help."

QUESTION: "My husband and I are new Christians. We have started praying with our young children, but we're not sure we are teaching them the right way to pray. How can we know if we are doing it right?"

ANSWER: "Remember that no one comes into this world knowing how to pray," writes my friend, Dr. Fisher Humphreys, well-known theological professor, author, and the father of grown children. "It's an activity that must be learned, and the best teachers are parents. Parents shouldn't worry too much about whether they are doing everything right. The principal things are to be sincere and simply to talk to God about what is on one's heart.

"The best way to teach anyone to pray is by example. If parents pray during difficult times, children will sense that this is a good thing to do. And it will be easier to pray during difficult times if parents have been praying routinely all along. Even a simple prayer at mealtimes is enough to accustom children to hearing their parents pray."

QUESTION: "My children's prayers sometimes seem silly and immature. Does this offend God?"
ANSWER: Children's prayers delight God! He cares about what they care about. As a child, I once asked Papa if I "should bother God with little things that are important to me." He smiled, his sky blue eyes glistening, and he said: "'Nisey, God cares so much about you that He counts the hairs on your head. You can talk with God about anything, big or small."

My friend and pastor's wife, Paulette Madkins, tells me: "I never coached my children in what to say, but I allowed them to be free to talk to God in their own way. I have seen as they get older and understand more, their prayers change."

Remember that Jesus lifted the children to his lap when his disciples tried to shoo them away. He even advised us adults to come to Him like little children. (See Matthew 18:1-5 NIV and read these verses to your children: "At that time the disciples came to Jesus and asked, 'Who is the greatest in the kingdom of heaven?' He called a little child and had him stand among them. And he said: 'I tell you the truth, unless you change and become like little children, you will never enter the kingdom of heaven. Therefore, whoever humbles himself like this child is the greatest in the kingdom of heaven. And whoever welcomes a little child like this in my name welcomes me.") God loves children, and He loves their prayers.

QUESTION: "How can we know for sure that God hears the prayers our family prays to Him and will respond?" ANSWER: Scripture tells us that: *God hears our prayers*: Listen to the Psalmists: "You hear, O Lord, the desire of the afflicted; You encourage them, and you listen to their cry..." (Psalm 10:17 NIV). "O you who hear prayer, to you all men will come" (Psalm 65:2). "...God has surely listened and heard my voice in prayer..." (Psalm 66:19 NIV). Jesus believed that God hears prayer. He prayed in front of Lazarus' tomb: "Father, I thank you that you have heard me. *I know that you always hear me*..." (John 11: 41-43). *God responds*: Again, the Psalmist writes: "Moses and Aaron were among his priests, Samuel was among those who called on his name; they called on the Lord and he answered them" (Psalm 99:6 NIV). "Then you will call, and the Lord will answer; you will cry for help, and he will say: 'Here am I'" (Isaiah 58:9 NIV).

QUESTION: "I am a Christian, but my husband does not believe in God. He tells me I can teach our children what I want about God, but he'll have no part in it. Can I teach my children to pray without his help?"

ANSWER: The ideal family prayer time, of course, includes all members of the family, especially the mother and father. But moms everywhere are teaching their children about God without help from a spouse. Pray especially for your husband and his salvation. My friend, Kathy, prayed for years that her husband would accept Christ and live for Him. Not until her two daughters became teenagers did he surrender his life to Jesus. With tears in her eyes, and with great joy, she now tells me how wonderful family devotions are with him and the girls. Never give up. God is always at work bringing unsaved fathers to Himself. Until then, make family devotions a priority in your home.

QUESTION: "My husband and I just became believers in Christ. We realize how important it is to teach our school-aged children to pray. But is it too late to start?"
ANSWER: It's never too late to start teaching children how to pray. Find a Bible-believing church that puts emphasis on its children's programs, and get your family involved. Choose Christian friends, of all ages, and spend time with them. Enlist help from Sunday School teachers, pastors, and other Christians who can help you teach your children about God and prayer. Have meaningful devotions each day as a family.

QUESTION: "Should we have our family devotions when friends drop by or are visiting?"
ANSWER: Yes! Include your friends, and your

children's friends, in your family devotional time. Just explain to them that each evening at this time you join together and read God's Word and pray. Invite them to join you as you and your family worship God.

QUESTION: "When is the best time to have family devotions?"

ANSWER: Some families have devotions at breakfast before everyone marches off into the day. If mornings aren't too rushed, and if your family is a "morning" family, then I believe that's the best time of day for devotions. But most families I talk with prefer evening devotions. They tell me they are more relaxed then. I find, however, that evening devotions can be interrupted by phone calls, unexpected visitors, school or church activities, and a host of other things that interrupt and separate family members. Discover what works best for your family. It's not really important when you worship together, but that you do it regularly.

QUESTION: "My children ask me all kinds of spiritual questions I cannot answer. What can I do?"

ANSWER: When Alyce or Christian ask me a question I can't answer, I refer them to my husband, Timothy. If Timothy is out of town and cannot be reached, I put them in touch with my Sunday School teacher, Jan Alsabrook, or our pastor, Danny Wood, or our senior pastor, Charles Carter. By surrounding yourself with mature Christian teachers and pastors and friends, someone is almost always available to help out. I also believe every family needs a good set of Bible commentaries. Digging in the Word for answers to spiritual questions is a great way to teach children about God's Word. It also teaches children how to find answers for their own spiritual questions. And kids can come up with some pretty tough questions!

QUESTION: "We've tried to have family devotions but our small children lose interest after a few minutes. Should we make them pay attention for our hour of devotions and punish them when they misbehave?"
ANSWER: It's hard for small children to sit still for an hour of devotions. You could shorten family prayer time to six or seven minutes. During that time, read a verse from the Bible, and follow it with a brief prayer. Prayer time should be good family time, not a time to discipline or punish. We want our children to look forward to our devotional time, not dread it. You can lengthen family prayer time as your children get older.

QUESTION: "What do the 'experts' say about family prayer and worship?"
ANSWER: One of my favorite experts on worship is Dr. Warren Wiersbe. Not only is he a talented author, but a good friend as well. In his book, *Family Worship,* he gives us some valuable insights about worship. "It must be regular, systematic, and flexible. Mother and

father must have their own personal 'quiet time' before they attempt to lead their children. One of the purposes for a family devotional time is to teach the children to have their own quiet time and to help to develop in them a desire for a daily fellowship with God. There must be variety and flexibility. As the children mature, the older ones can assist in the reading and praying. While it must not be a 'fun time,' it should be enjoyable. Our practice was to gear the reading to the youngest member of the family, whose attention span was much shorter than ours. ...Each family must determine when is the best time for the family altar. At one stage in our lives, after breakfast was the ideal time. Later, with changing school schedules, it was more convenient immediately after supper. There were some days when the schedule fell apart and we had no devotional time at all with the children. But we did not feel guilty; we just picked it up the next day and kept on going. By the way, when you and the family are driving down the highway, you have a wonderful opportunity for an impromptu family altar. The spontaneous devotional times can carry more variety – spontaneity – flexibility: those would be the characteristics of a successful family altar."[58]

QUESTION: "We don't have time to pray as a family. What do other busy families do?"
ANSWER: Lack of family time rates high on today's families' list of everyday complaints. Every family I

know seems to be running in all directions just to keep up with life and laundry and living expenses! A few days ago, I emailed my sister, Jill: "Greetings, Jill! Your day sounds something like my day! One wonders how we ever survive the work and chaos of a single day! This evening, Christian has a soccer game half way across town; Alyce has a football game and dinner with friends after her guitar lesson; and Timothy and I are hosting a dinner downtown for some colleagues. Tomorrow looks even busier. You know, life is kind of funny when I start to think about it. I go from a pile of dirty laundry, to an evening out, to calling the plumber to unstop the sink, to a Christian ladies' luncheon, to picking up kids from school, to rushing to a church meeting, to serving refreshments at a soccer game... you get the idea. I put on hose and heels, then change to sneakers, put on hose and heels, then change to sneakers. I should be dizzy by now! When I get a moment to stop, catch my breath, and look around, I notice that at least half the light bulbs in the house have burned out, something seems to have died in the refrigerator, and at least two out of the three toilets are stopped up! And the cats look skinnier than usual! And my flowers have been overwhelmed by weeds! Well, must run now. Got to make supper and wash a load of clothes and pick up children from school. Hope you have a good weekend. Denise."

Sometimes it seems impossible to gather as a family for prayer and Scripture reading. But, when I am the busiest, I try to remind myself that teaching children about prayer, and praying together as a family, is the most important thing I'll ever do for my children. Prayer has somehow got to be our priority. Again, Dr. Wiersbe writes: "...Start each day with God – not reading a quick verse-prayer-and-poem devotional, but spending time in His Word, in meditation and worship, and in prayer. Time. That is where the rub comes in. We do not 'take time to be holy.' We are satisfied with 'religious fast food' that is packaged for quick and easy consumption. Perhaps 'fast food' is better than nothing at all, but is a poor substitute for the real thing. True worship takes time, and one of the evidences that we are starting to make spiritual progress in our worship is the calmness that comes to the soul as you wait before God. You are conscious of time but not controlled by time. You enjoy waiting before the Lord and reveling in His wonder and His greatness."[59]

Give prayer time all the time you can. The more time, the better. While a little time is better than no time at all, I must agree with Dr. Wiersbe. I must also agree with Samuel Chadwick who says: "Hurry is the death of prayer." When weekdays prove too hectic for "waiting before the Lord and reveling in His wonder and His greatness," plan a special devotional time – at weekends or holidays – when your family can spend more time "in His Word, in meditation and worship, and in prayer. "

QUESTION: "What is meant by 'listening to God.' Do you really 'hear' His voice speak to you?"

ANSWER: God speaks to us in many ways. How important it is to teach our children to listen, as well as to talk to God! God speaks to us when we read the Bible. God often speaks to us through nature or events or circumstances. God speaks to our hearts, not in an audible voice, (although I believe He can if He desires to), and directs us in our decisions. His Spirit speaks to our Spirit – deep unto deep – in mystery, the mystery that passes our understanding.

QUESTION: "My children act like brats! I am fed up with trying to teach them anything, spiritual or otherwise. Do other parents have such problems with their kids?"

ANSWER: Yes, they do. At times, all children can act like brats! It's necessary to remember that children "act" like brats, but that, in themselves, they are precious children loved by God. We can still love the children, while we strongly dislike their behavior. I love what C. S. Lewis says about kids. He writes: "But every child is sometimes infuriating; most children are not infrequently odious. ...but in everyone, and of course in ourselves, there is that which requires forbearance, tolerance, forgiveness."[60]

How true! I didn't know the meaning of "tolerance" and "forbearance" and "forgiveness" until I had children! Before I had children, I often prayed for more patience. God surely heard my prayer because when He delivered Christian and Alyce to us, we quickly learned patience, and tolerance, forbearance, and forgiveness, too!

Mark Twain once jokingly gave his advice on children. He wrote: "When a child turns thirteen, put him in a barrel and feed him through the hole; when he turns sixteen, plug up the hole."[61]

Not long ago, my friend, Sara Beard, a mother of young adults, asked me a question: "Denise," she said, "do you know why Abraham agreed to sacrifice Isaac when Isaac was twelve years old?" I knew a trick answer would follow. "Because," she continued, "if Isaac had been thirteen, it wouldn't have been a sacrifice!"

While it is fun to laugh at "teenager" jokes, especially if we've "been there," we must never give up on them – even when they "act" like brats!

QUESTION: "I feel I have been a failure as a Christian parent. I have put everything else ahead of my children's spiritual teachings. We never prayed together, and rarely went to church. My children are teenagers now and neither has made a personal commitment to Christ. They are uninterested in religion. Is it too late to influence them for Christ?"

ANSWER: We all fail at one time or another. That's part of being human. I keep the following quote on my computer to remind me that God forgives failures, and that's it is never too late to pick ourselves up, dust ourselves off, ask for forgiveness, and get on with our God-given parental tasks: "A study of Bible characters," writes Dr. Oswald Sanders, "reveals that most of those who made history were men who failed at some point, and some of them drastically, but who refused to continue lying in the dust. Their very failure and repentance secured to them a more ample conception of the grace of God. They learned to know Him as the God of the second chance to His children who had failed Him – and the third chance, too."[62]

QUESTION: "My two children 'fight' all the time. How can our family have a time of quiet, orderly devotions when we have to referee our kids like boxers in a ring?" ANSWER: My children fought with each other all the time, too! One day, after I had spent the entire morning as Mother Referee for my two hair-pulling, doll-swiping, small-fry opponents, my friend called me on the phone. I was almost in tears. "Sometimes it's so hard to be a mother," I confessed. I'll never forget her words to me. "Denise," she said, "just open yourself to God and let Him mother through you. After all, they're His kids." As the mother of teenagers, I still try to remember her words - my children are ultimately God's children. I am a caretaker (or referee) for a few years, but they belong to God eternally.

I did and God did. That morning I learned that, ultimately, God is responsible for the outcome of my children. For they are His children. I am just a trusted caretaker who, for a little while, is given the ministry of parenting for Him.

Pray together with your children about this problem that divides your family. Read to them some of the Biblical stories about the results of sibling rivalry. (See the following examples of sibling rivalry and read them to your children:

Abimelech, Jotham and brothers: Judges 9:1-57.

Absalom, Amnon, and Tamar: 2 Samuel 13:1-39.

Cain and Abel: Genesis 4:1-11.

David and Eliab: 1 Samuel 17:28-30.

Er and Onan: Genesis 38:1-10.

Jacob and Esau: Genesis 25:22-28:9; 32:1-33:17; Malachi 1:2-3.

Joseph and brothers: Genesis 37, 39-50.

Leah and Rachel: Genesis 29:16-30:24.

Moses, Aaron, and Miriam: Numbers. 12:1-15.

Prodigal son and older brother: Luke 15:25-30.

Shem, Ham, and Japheth: Genesis 9:20-27.

Solomon and Adonijah: 1 Kings 1:5-53.

If the fighting continues, separate them. Try a one-on-one prayer time until they agree to get along. Read up on what some "experts" write about sibling rivalry. And, by the way...Good luck!

QUESTION: "My son seems very shy about praying in front of our family members. Our other children are eager to pray, but he refuses to take part. When I call on him to lead the family prayer, he looks at the floor and shakes his head. Should I make him pray?"

ANSWER: Some people are shy about expressing themselves in prayer in public. Author Michael Card makes an interesting statement about public prayer: "...If you really want to know someone's heart, listen to them pray. Prayer is the truest way to reveal yourself, not only to God, but to those around you. Perhaps that's why so many of us are reluctant to lead prayer in public. We do not want to be discovered."[63]

Don't force your son to pray or to lead in prayer. Some children suffer from extreme shyness; others want to keep their thoughts private. Try holding hands and sitting in a circle during family prayer time. Instead of having a prayer leader, go around the circle and let all those who want to pray say a sentence prayer. This may encourage your shy son to participate.

QUESTION: "I prayed with my children, and now my children have children. How can I best pray for and with my grandchildren?"

ANSWER: My good friend, Irene Endicott, answers this question in her wonderful new book, *Grandparenting: It's Not What It Used to Be*!

• "Pray for your grandchildren before they are conceived. Ask God to make you into the grandparent they will need."

• "As the baby grows, pray for the baby's healthy development, physically, spiritually, and emotionally. Pray for wisdom and a special sensitivity toward this child."

• "Thank God for protecting the infant and for giving the child a sense of security and well-being and a responsive heart toward Him."

• "Pray in your grandchildren's rooms at their home. When you visit, step into their rooms and pray. God's presence can fill a place so that it affects what happens there."

• "Ask God to bring your grandchildren to mind whenever they need help. As you think of them, stop for a moment of prayer, prompted by the Holy Spirit. The more you do this, the more you will sense what they need and how to pray for them."

• "Don't force a grandchild to pray in your world. First Corinthians 13:11 says that when you are a child, you think as one. Pray in their world. Pray about things that are important to them...."

• "Pray *with* them rather than *at* them. If prayer is used as a means of discipline, children won't want to pray."

• "Teach them to pray for others' needs, praying until the answer comes. Give thanks with them when God answers. Share your prayer needs with them. This forms a strong bond between you as they pray for you and realize that you value their prayers."

• "Pray for the healing of their spirits. Ask God to help you be sensitive to their hurts and to see it from their perspective. Pray for God to touch their hurt and heal it, so hurts do not build up."

• "If your grandchildren are adopted or foster children,

pray for every part of their lives before they became part of your family."

• Believe in their spiritual potential. Grandparents can make a big difference as they recognize and affirm their grandchildren's gifts and help develop them."

• "Look for opportunities for spontaneous prayer with your grandchildren. It could well be the moment in their day that gets them through their day."[64]

QUESTION: "I like to hold hands as a family when we pray. But my sixteen-year-old son won't have any part of it. In fact, he never wants me to hug him or touch him at all. What should I do?"

ANSWER: My children have also reached this "untouchable" teenage stage of life! As a youngster, Alyce lived in my lap. She wanted to hug and kiss me all the time. When we walked, she held my hand. When I dropped her off at school, she'd reach up for a lengthy, neck-squeezing hug. When she sat next to me in church, she kept both arms tightly around me. Then she hit her teens, and all of a sudden, she doesn't want to touch me anymore. You'd think that overnight I had contracted the Bubonic Plague.

Prayer techniques should change as children grow older. If your child no longer wants to hold hands during prayer, find another way to pray. But, meaningful touch is important to everyone. Whenever I can, I hug my teenagers and give them a pat on the back. They don't always like it, and nine times out of ten they will pull away. But I simply tell them: "Guys, get used to it. That's what mothers do."

I like what author Randy Carlson writes: "Meaningful touch is so important that one recent research study found that it takes eight to ten 'meaningful touches' daily to maintain proper emotional and physical health.... To meaningfully touch a child or teenager...doesn't require a ten-minute, bone-crushing embrace. Sometimes it just means an affectionate pat on the shoulder or a squeeze of the hand."[65]

QUESTION: "How does God want to be loved?"
ANSWER: God wants us to love Him with everything we have. Heart, soul, and mind. (Read often the following scripture to your children: Matthew 22:37: "Jesus replied: 'Love the Lord your God with all your heart and with all your soul and with all your mind. This is the first and greatest commandment" NIV). Author Walter Trobisch puts it this way: "God wants to be loved as a father and a mother are loved by their children, as a friend by a friend, as a man by his wife and a wife by her husband, as a sick person by a caring nurse and as a guest by his host. God finds great joy when we express our feelings toward Him."[66]

Family worship gives us ample opportunities to express our love for God and to God.
QUESTION: "I am a single mom with three school-aged children. I hold down two jobs, and I'm just

hoping to meet the bills and survive. God hasn't been my priority, and we don't have family prayer. But I do try to take my children to church regularly. Are my children getting all they need spiritually?

ANSWER: Motherhood is an unbelievably difficult job even in the best, two-parent situations. It seems to me that single motherhood is an almost impossible job! I cannot even imagine the responsibilities single moms have with children, home, and outside employment. I marvel at my single mother friends who juggle six balls in the air all the time without dropping one of them! I'm glad to hear that you take your children to church, and that you care about their spiritual development. But I believe taking them to church isn't enough. Spiritual teaching in the home is too important to delegate it to the church. Tim Kimmel writes: "Kids need to receive a depth of spiritual wisdom to turn to when needed. The best way to do this is by modeling our own spiritual growth and surrounding ourselves with mentors who can help us wisely lead our children. Kids need to be taught how to pray, how to find their way around the Bible, and how to get the most out of their church experience."[67]

For single parents, extra time may not exist. Look at your daily schedule. See where you can find a few extra minutes a day. List your priorities. Teaching your children to love God and pray, bonding together during family devotions should be very high, if not number one, on your list. Finding time may mean simply getting up ten minutes earlier in the mornings.

Ask mature Christians in the church to help you teach your children about spiritual things. Children respond well to a Christian mentor, especially if that person teaches their Sunday school class.

QUESTION: "How does praying together as a family affect our children's lives and also the lives of others?" ANSWER: Let me answer this last question with a personal example: Picture a group of feisty twelve-year-old boys clad in soccer gear, standing in the rain, huddled in a circle. The state championship soccer tournament is about to begin. My son stands among his rugged teammates. Raindrops and sweat drip off their downy "man-child" faces; butterflies frolic in their stomachs; their shuffling feet anxiously await the big kick-off. But for a brief moment, their heads are bowed; their eyes are closed.

As is his pre-game habit, Coach Emmanuel Chekwa, the volunteer Christian coach for the "Briarwood Ambassadors," asks: "Okay boys. Let's pray. Who wants to pray?" Ten hands shoot up. Coach Chekwa chooses my son, Christian, to lead the team in prayer.

Tears come as I stand on the sidelines and listen to my young son's prayer. With no hesitation or embarrassment, Christian prays for the sportsmanship and safety of both teams. He prays for Coach. He speaks as naturally to God as if He is a well-known, much-loved friend.

I must admit that I don't remember which team won that championship. The complicated rules of soccer still confuse me. But I'll never forget my son's words that day when he so freely and so naturally talked to God on that rain-soaked soccer field.

You see, when families pray together in the home, their sons and daughters take those prayers out into the world. Whatever children learn at home, they take with them into society. They do this naturally because the home is their first training ground.

How sad when this concept works in a negative way. Consider what happens when parents use bad language at home. The children will naturally use bad language themselves. When a parent smokes cigarettes, the child will be inclined to also smoke cigarettes. The same is true with alcohol or drugs. If a mother or father abuse alcohol or drugs, chances are greater that the child will follow in those chemically-abusive footsteps. A child who is abused by his father in the home will more than likely become a child abuser himself. A parent who conveniently cheats and lies will produce cheating and lying children. Children learn how to conduct themselves in public, children learn the values they take into life, and children learn how to relate to others, from what their parents teach them at home.

When parents teach their children to pray, pray with them regularly in the home, and live a prayer-filled life, children will consider prayer a natural part of everyday life. This is especially true when parents start praying early with their young children.

The boys on Christian's soccer team all had praying parents, thus ten hands shot up when Coach asked someone to pray. That night, they were all little "soccer-clad" lights shining in a very dark world.

***

Surely, we must teach our children to pray!

FOOTNOTES

1   (Timothy and Denise George, *Dear Unborn Child*, Nashville, TN: Broadman Press, 1984, p. 17-18.)

2   (Tim Kimmel, *Raising Kids Who Turn Out Right*, Sisters, OR: Multnomah, 1989/1993, p. 52.)

3   (Oswald Chambers, *My Utmost for His Highest* New York: Dodd, Mead, and Co., 1935, p. 147.)

4   (Tim Kimmel, *Raising Kids Who Turn Out Right*, Sisters, OR: Multnomah, 1989/1993, p. 58.)

5   ("Debbie Smith, Number One on Michael's Chart" by Pamela Nixon, quoted from *Journey,* Nashville, TN: BSSB, May 1996)

6   ("Debbie Smith, Number One on Michael's Chart" by Pamela Nixon, quoted from *Journey,* Nashville, TN: BSSB, May 1996)

7   (Tim Kimmel, *Raising Kids Who Turn Out Right*, Sisters, OR: Multnomah, 1989/1993, p. 56.)

8   ("The Private World of Bill Gates: A Surprising Visit with the Man Who is Shaping Our Future," *Time,* Jan. 13, 1997, p. 51.)

9   (James Dobson, *Solid Answers*, Wheaton, IL: Tyndale House Publishers, Inc., 1997, p. 211.)

10 (Charles Colson, *A Dance With Deception*, Dallas, TX: Word Publishing, 1993, p. 77.)

11 (Joe White, *Faithtraining: Raising Kids Who Love the Lord*, Colorado Springs, CO: Focus On the Family Publishing, 1994, p. 305).

12 (Walter Scott, "Personality Parade," *Parade Magazine*, The Birmingham News, Sunday, Sept. 28, 1997, p. 1.)

13 (Joe White, *Faithtraining: Raising Kids Who Love the Lord*, Colorado Springs, CO: Focus On the Family Publishing, 1994, p. 84).

14 (Charles Colson, "Quoting the Bible Isn't Enough," *Christianity Today:* August 11, 1997, p. 72.)

15 (Denise George, "Silver and Gold I Have," *Contempo*, Aug. 1991, p. 2.)

16 (Tom Wright, *The Original Jesus*, Grand Rapids, MI: William B. Eerdmans Pub. Co., 1996, p. 111.)

17 (R. G. Lee, *PayDay Someday*, Denise & Timothy George, general editors, *Library of Baptist Classic Series*, Nashville, TN: Broadman/Holman, 1995, p. 198.)

18 (Philip Yancey, *The Jesus I Never Knew,* Grand Rapids, MI: Zondervan Publishing House, 1995, p. 94-95).

[19] (Philip Yancey, *The Jesus I Never Knew*, Grand Rapids, MI: Zondervan Publishing House, 1995, p. 95.)

[20] (Margaret Wise Brown, *The Runaway Bunny*, HarperTrophy Publishers, 1942; 1970; 1972; 1982, no page numbers.)

[21] (Carla Caldwell, "Baby Hope," *Birmingham News*, 2 Mar. 1989. Quoted from Denise George, *Becoming Tender In a Tough World* Nashville: Broadman Press, 1990, pp. 151-152).

[22] (Gary Smalley & John Trent, "The Blessing," Nashville, TN: Thomas Nelson Publishers, 1986, p. 77.)

[23] Young children may have trouble with slaughtering innocent lambs. Consider their ages when telling these Bible stories. A young child may hear this as being cruel to animals. An older child can be helped to understand the meaning. I believe we cannot explain the sacrifice of Jesus on the cross, our redemption, forgiveness of sins, and atonement unless we provide this explanation.

[24] (W. Phillip Keller. *A Gardener Looks at the Fruits of the Spirit*. Waco, TX: Word Books, 1979, p. 61, emphasis mine.)

[25] (Phillip Keller, *A Shepherd Looks at the Good Shepherd and His Sheep*, Grand Rapids, MI: Zondervan Publishing House, 1978, p. 165.)

[26] (Henri J. M. Nouwen, *The Way of the Heart*, New York: Ballantine Books, 1981, p. 53.)

[27] (Marie Dawson, "Against the Tide," *Christianity Today*, Nov. 13, 1995, p. 43).

[28] (Phillip Keller, *Sea Edge*, (Waco, TX: Word Books, 1985), p. 83.)

[29] (Dan Allender, *Bold Love*. Colorado Springs, CO: NavPress, 1992, p. 66).

[30] (John A. Broadus, *Baptist Confessions, Covenants, and Catechisms*, Timothy and Denise George, Editors; *The Library of Baptist Classics*, "A Catechism for Babes, or, Little Ones, (1652)," (Nashville, TN: Broadman/Holman Publishers, 1996, pp. 127 and 239).

[31] (James Dobson, *When God Doesn't Make Sense*, Wheaton, IL: Tyndale House Publishers, Inc., 1993, p. 100.)

[32] (T.W. Hunt, *The Mind of Christ*, Nashville, TN: Broadman/Holman, 1995, p. 98.)

[33] "Although a very rare phenomenon, bloody sweat (hematidrosis or hemohidrosis) may occur in highly emotional states or in persons with bleeding disorders.

As a result of hemorrhage into the sweat glands, the skin becomes fragile and tender. Luke's description supports the diagnosis of hematidrosis rather than eccrine chromidrosis (brown or yellow-green sweat) or stigmatization (blood oozing from the palms or elsewhere). (William D. Edwards, MD; Wesley J. Gabel, MDIV; Floyd E. Hosmer, MS.AMI, "On the Physical Death of Jesus Christ," *JAMA (The Journal of the American Medical Association*, March 21, 1986, Vol. 255, No. 11, p. 1457.)

[34] (James Dobson, *When God Doesn't Make Sense,* Wheaton, IL: Tyndale House Publishers, Inc., 1993, p. 102.)

[35] (Philip Yancey, *The Jesus I Never Knew*, Grand Rapids, MI: Zondervan Publishing House, 1995, p, 161.)

[36] (W. Phillip Keller. *A Gardener Looks at the Fruits of the Spirit*, Waco, TX: Word Books, 1979, p. 69.)

[37] (John M. Todd, *Luther: A Life,* New York: Crossroad, 1982, p. 327).

[38] (Oswald Chambers, *My Utmost for His Highest,* New York: Dodd, Mead, and Co., 1935, p. 90.)

[39] (Patrick Johnstone, *Operation World*, England: WEC Publications and STL Books, 1978, p. 21. Note: *Operation World* is also available in a youth edition.)

[40] (Austin Phelps, *The Still Hours*, Carlisle, PA: The Banner of Truth Trust, 1974 [first published in 1859], p. 80).

[41] (Oswald Chambers, *If You Will Ask*, Grand Rapids, MI: Discovery House Publishers, 1958, p. 172.)

[42] (Warren Wiersbe, *Real Worship*, Nashville, TN: Oliver Nelson, 1986, p. 130.)

[43] (Gloria Gaither and Shirley Dobson, *Let's Make a Memory*, Waco, TX: Word Books, 1983, p. 183.)

[44] (Idea quoted from Debbie Caldwell Whisenant, "Family Activities," *Homelife Magazine*, Feb. 1996, np.)

[45] (Cindy McCormick Martinusen, "Learning Curve—A+ Prayers," *Homelife Magazine* Nashville, TN: BSSB, 1997, p. 62. Used with permission of the author.)

[46] (Keith Wooden, *Teaching Children to Pray*, Grand Rapids, MI: Zondervan Publishing House, 1992, p. 91.)

[47] (Elisabeth Elliot, *A Chance to Die: the Life and Legacy of Amy Carmichael*, Old Tappan, NJ: Fleming H. Revell co., 1987, p. 294.)

[48] (Henry Blackaby, *Discover,* B'ham, AL: Shades Mountain Baptist church, Sept. 19, 1997, p. 1)

[49] (Denise George, "A Time to Cry," *Contempo*, November 1989.)

[50] (Denise George, "God's Heart, God's Hands," *Journey*, April 1994, np.)

[51] (Denise George, "The Christmas Pageant," *Homelife Magazine*, 1990, p. 28.)

[52] (Walter Trobisch, preface, *I Loved a Girl*, NY: Harper & Row, Publishers, 1963).

[53] (Used by permission of author, Christian Timothy George, copyright 1991).

[54] (*The Freedom Fighter* by Derick Bingham published by Christian Focus Publications ISBN: 1-85792-3715)

[55] (Published by Christian Focus: *George Müller: The Children's Champion* Irene Howat, ISBN: 1-85792-5491; *Adoniram Judson: Danger on the Streets of Gold* Irene Howat, ISBN: 1-85792-6609; *Gladys Aylward: No Mountain too High* Myrna Grant, ISBN: 1-85792-5947)

[56] Christian Focus *Lightkeepers* series covers a variety of Christians such as Jonathan Edwards; David Livingstone; Joni Eareckson; Amy Carmichael; Corrie ten Boom.

[57] (Michael A. Mitchell, "Building a Strong Family," "Stand Firm: God's Challenge for Today's Man," Nashville, TN: Lifeway Press, Oct. 1997, p. 25.)

[58] (Warren Wiersbe, *Real Worship*, Nashville, TN: Oliver Nelson, 1986,p. 181-182.)

[59] (Warren Wiersbe, *Real Worship*, Nashville, TN: Oliver Nelson, 1986, p. 163)

[60] (C. S. Lewis, *The Four Loves*, New York, NY: Harcourt Barce Jovanovich, Publishers, 1960/1988, p. 135).

[61] (Keith Wooden, *Teaching Children to Pray*, Grand Rapids, MI: Zondervan Publishing House, 1992, p. 97.)

[62] (Oswald Sanders, *Spiritual Leadership*, Chicago, IL: Moody Press, 1967/1980, p. 163.)

[63] (Michael Card, *The Parable of Joy, Reflections on the Wisdom of the Book of John,* Nashville, TN: Thomas Nelson Publishers, 1995, p. 201.)

[64] (Irene Endicott, *Grandparenting: It's Not What It Used to Be!*, Nashville, TN: Broadman & Holman Publishers, 1997, p. 59-60, used with permission from the author.)

[65] (Randy Carlson, *The Cain and Abel Syndrome*, Nashville, TN: Thomas Nelson Publishers, 1994, p. 90.)

[66] (Walter, Trobisch, *All a Man Can Be*, Downers Grove, IL: InterVarsity Press, 1983, p. 77.)

[67] (Tim Kimmel, *Powerful Personalities*, Colorado Springs, CO: Focus On the Family, 1993, p. 170).

These books should be on every parent's shelf. With simple questions and answers, well chosen bible verses and helpful comments you will wonder how you managed without them.

My first book of questions and answers
ISBN 1-85792-570X
My first book of memory verses
ISBN 1-85792-7834
My first book of bible prayers ISBN 1-85792-944-6

Do you want to learn about God and how to please him?Do you want to learn about how to pray? Do you want to be part of this amazing adventure? *Then* This book is for you!

ISBN 1-85792-840-7

Aren't they lovely when they're asleep? – This is no dry Bible study that looks at principles without any grounding in reality, the author takes six key concepts: *accept, beware, communicate, discipline, evaluate* and *fear the Lord* and expands on them with practical advice and understanding sensitivity. A parenting book with Biblical authority and easy to understand application!

ISBN 1-85792-876-8

Of Such is the Kingdom – Timothy Sisemore builds a practical approach to parenting and children's ministry and shows how to nurture children to be disciples. This is not a theoretical book - if you recognize the need to change your approach he shows you how to do that.

ISBN 1-85792-514-9

Christian Focus Publications

We publish books for all ages. Our mission statement –

STAYING FAITHFUL

In dependence upon God we seek to help make His infallible Word, the Bible, relevant. Our aim is to ensure that the Lord Jesus Christ is presented as the only hope to obtain forgiveness of sin, live a useful life and look forward to heaven with Him.

REACHING OUT

Christ's last command requires us to reach out to our world with His gospel. We seek to help fulfill that by publishing books that point people towards Jesus and help them develop a Christ-like maturity. We aim to equip all levels of readers for life, work, ministry and mission.

Books in our adult range are published in three imprints.

Christian Focus contains popular works including biographies, commentaries, basic doctrine and Christian living. Our children's books are also published in this imprint.

Christian Heritage contains classic writings from the past.

Mentor focuses on books written at a level suitable for Bible College and seminary students, pastors, and other serious readers. The imprint includes commentaries, doctrinal studies, examination of current issues and church history.

We can be contacted at:

Christian Focus Publications Ltd
Geanies House, Fearn,
Ross-shire, IV20 1TW, Scotland,
United Kingdom
info@christianfocus.com

For details of our titles visit us on our website
www.christianfocus.com